PATHS, STEPS & PATIOS

FOR THE GARDEN

STEP-BY-STEP PRACTICAL GUIDES

PATHS, STEPS & PATIOS

FOR THE GARDEN

Including 16 easy-to-build projects

ALAN & GILL BRIDGEWATER

Published by Silverdale Books
an imprint of Bookmart Ltd in 2005

Bookmart Ltd
Blaby Road, Wigston
Leicester LE18 4SE

Registered Number 2372865

ISBN 1 84509 355 0

Editorial Direction: Rosemary Wilkinson
Project Editor: Clare Johnson
Production: Hazel Kirkman

Designed and created for New Holland by AG&G BOOKS
Designer: Glyn Bridgewater
Illustrator: Gill Bridgewater
Project design: Alan and Gill Bridgewater
Photography: AG&G Books and Ian Parsons
Editor: Fiona Corbridge
Project construction: Alan and Gill Bridgewater

Reproduction by Pica Digital, Singapore
Printed and bound in Malaysia by Times Offset (M) Sdn. Bhd.

Contents

Introduction 6

Part 1: Techniques 8

Designing and planning 10
Tools 12
Materials 16
Foundations 20
Brickwork and stonework techniques 22
Woodwork techniques 24
Paths 26
Patios 28
Steps 30

Part 2: Projects 32

Decking tile patio 34
Zigzag brick border path 38
Woodland steps 42
Rustic log ring path 46
Inspirations: Paths 50
Natural patio 52
Green wood walkway 56
Classic stone sett patio 62
Art Deco steps 68
Inspirations: Steps 74
Elizabethan half-circle doorstep 76
Decorative Victorian path 82
Railway sleeper steps 88
Semicircular herb walk 94
Crazy-paved circular patio 100
Inspirations: Patios 106
Snake-pattern cobble path 108
Raised decking 114
Wooden stairway 120

Glossary 126
Suppliers 126
Conversion chart 127
Index 128

Introduction

When we were first married, we moved to an isolated, tumbledown cottage in the country. It was bliss – just the two of us... and two dogs, a cat, a couple of goats, two geese and a hen. The garden was huge, with lots of apple trees and some derelict stone and brick outhouses. Though it was "romantic" struggling through the long, wet grass and mud to the well, and scrambling up the slope to the chicken house to retrieve eggs, we soon decided that we needed order. The first job was to pull down the outhouses and clear the bricks and stones. The next step was to build a brick path from the house to the well. Then we constructed a flight of steps up the bank to the chicken house.

Soon we were busy building projects for family and friends – a red brick path for Gill's parents, a flight of railway sleeper steps for my brother, a vast decking patio for a family who lived by the river. Each project was an exciting new adventure. The starting point was to find out what our clients envisaged, and whether they had been inspired by something they had seen. We discussed the construction options, and whether old or new materials were preferred. Then we wandered around the site exploring the possibilities and taking

measurements, before establishing the final position for the project and working on the design. An added benefit of all these commissions was that we made friends with many local suppliers.

Building paths, steps and patios in the garden is wonderful fun. If you enjoy working with bricks, stone, wood, mortar and concrete, and are looking for a challenge, you are going to a get a great deal of pleasure from this book, and will learn some useful skills.

Best of luck.

Alan & Gill

HEALTH AND SAFETY

Many stone, brick and woodworking procedures are potentially dangerous, so before starting work on the projects, check through the following list:

- Make sure that you are fit and strong enough for the task ahead. If you have doubts, ask your doctor for specific advice.
- When you are lifting large lumps of stone from ground level, minimize back strain by bending your knees, hugging the stone close to your body, and keeping the spine upright.
- If a slab of stone or baulk of wood looks too heavy to lift on your own, find a better way of moving it – with a sack barrow, roller or pulley – or ask others to help.
- Wear gloves, a dust-mask and goggles when you are handling cement and lime, cutting stone with a hammer and chisel, using the angle grinder, or sanding wood that has been treated with preservatives.
- Never operate a power tool such as an angle grinder, drill or jigsaw, or attempt a difficult lifting or manoeuvring task, if you are feeling tired or are under medication.
- Keep a first-aid kit and telephone within easy reach, in case of emergencies.

Part 1: **Techniques**

Designing and planning

As with so many ventures in life, a successful garden feature is made up of one part inspiration, one part perspiration, and two parts organization. Be prepared to spend time thinking carefully about all the implications of a project, from taking measurements to considering how much help you are going to need – it will pay off. Arm yourself with a notebook and pencil, and start your advance planning campaign.

FIRST CONSIDERATIONS

- Do you live in an area where there are reliable sources of supply, such as builders' merchants and salvage companies?
- Will local companies deliver small quantities of stone and wood, or are you going to fetch the materials yourself – if so will you need to hire a trailer or a truck?
- Is there adequate, safe access to your garden – a wide gateway, and room for trucks to turn?
- How are you going to move the delivered materials to the site? Are you going to do it yourself or ask friends to help?
- Is there a sawmill in the area, where you can buy a good range of rough-sawn and pre-treated wood?
- Do children and pets use your garden, and if so, is their presence going to affect your choice of project?
- Where are you going to do the woodwork? Are you going to work on a patio, in a yard, or on the lawn?
- Are any of your neighbours going to be concerned about the siting of a project, to the extent that you need to involve them at the planning stage? Consultation prevents conflict!
- Is your garden reasonably level and dry? Or is it swampy with soft, squashy lawns and stony outcrops? If so, what measures will you need to take to provide suitable areas to build on?

Choosing a suitable project

When you have decided what you want to build in general terms, you to need to focus in on the details. You must consider all the aspects of your chosen project to determine whether it is suitable for the size and location of your garden and, of course, the size of your bank balance. You also need to assess whether you are strong enough for the work involved.

Let's say, for example, that you have chosen to build the Raised Decking (see page 114) with the Wooden Stairway (see page 120). Will you need to modify the size and shape of the decking to fit the available space? Is the decking going to look right in your garden? Is it suitable for your children? Will it upset your neighbours – for instance will it overlook their garden? Are you going to have to move plants in readiness for building the decking? Or could you perhaps leave plants to grow through and around the finished decking? Does the number of steps in the stairway need to be adjusted to suit the slope of the ground?

Planning the project

Once you are clear about all the implications of building your chosen project, you need to plan out the logistics. When are you going to start building? Are you going to run it over several weekends, or are you going to start work during a longer holiday period? If you have put aside a specific weekend and are counting on the supplier to deliver the materials then, are you sure that the supplier is able to oblige? Would it be better to order the materials to be delivered well in advance?

Do you require the help of some friends to complete the project, and if so, will you need to obtain additional tools for them to use? Don't forget that your helpers will probably also need feeding during the course of the day, so you need to buy provisions and sort out catering arrangements.

Will adverse weather cause difficulties? If you have to lay concrete, rain will hold you up unless you cover the area with a tarpaulin. Will it matter if you run a wheelbarrow repeatedly over your lawn? Heavy loads will inevitably damage the grass and create a muddy valley, so you may prefer to lay boards to avoid this. Will it be necessary to hire extra items such as another wheelbarrow or a concrete mixer? Are the children going to be a help or a hindrance? Maybe they should stay with friends for the day. Every detail needs to be planned out, from the minute the materials arrive to the moment when the project is ready to use.

Buying the right tools and materials

Though we have suggested using certain tools, you can of course make changes to suit your individual requirements. For example, instead of investing in a pair of portable workbenches, you could save money by using a couple of upturned tea chests. Much the same goes for the materials: if you would prefer to modify the project, such as by using salvaged bricks rather than new, or a different grade and size of wood, that is your choice. Most of the projects are flexible enough to accommodate such changes.

The quantities specified are generally very generous, especially for sand and cement. It is much better to finish up with a surplus than to run out of cement when you are halfway through laying a concrete slab and the shops are closed. When ordering materials, phone around for quotes, and ask if there are any bargains such as end-of-line items, or special offers. We always order well in advance, and pay on delivery. On no account part with money until the materials are on your property and you have checked them over for quality and quantity.

PATH, STEP AND PATIO DESIGNS FOR THE GARDEN

LEFT This garden plan demonstrates how the projects in this book might be used to fill your garden with attractive paths, steps and patios.

Tools

While you can cut costs by using tools that are less than perfect – such as a saw that is not quite the right type, or a spade that is too short – a carefully considered tool will cut down on time and effort and make the task all the more enjoyable. A basic tool kit for the projects in this book is described below.

TOOLS FOR MEASURING AND MARKING

Spirit level

Tape measure

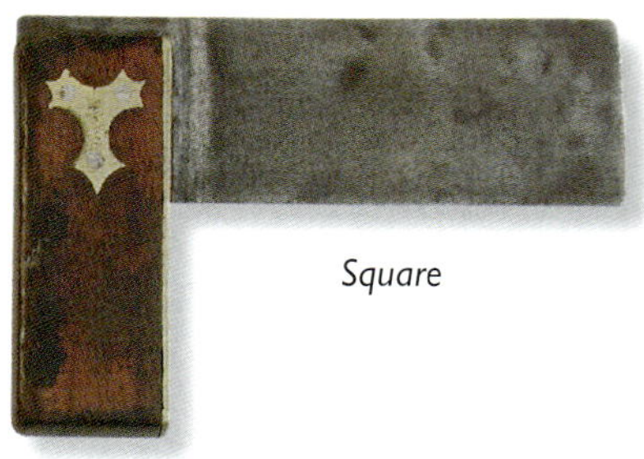

Square

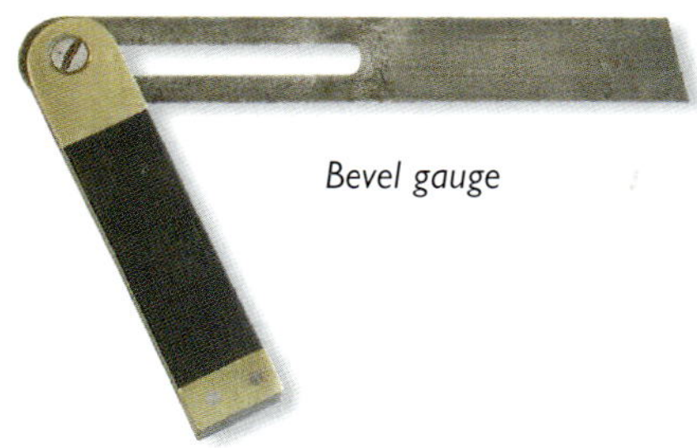

Bevel gauge

Carpenter's pencil

Measuring and marking out the site

You need a flexible tape measure for setting out the site plan, wooden pegs for markers, string to delineate the shape of the foundation or footings, and chalk. A fibreglass tape measure is a good investment because it is waterproof and stands up well to the dirt, wear and tear involved in garden projects.

Woodworking tools for measuring and marking

We use four tools: a tape measure for establishing lengths and widths, a square for setting out right angles, a bevel gauge for angles that are bigger or smaller than 90°, and a carpenter's pencil. If we need a straight-edge, we generally use a length of timber. A small steel rule is handy for marking out joints.

Levelling

You need a long-bodied spirit level for checking the correctness of vertical and horizontal surfaces. If you intend to build a lot of projects, buy one made of wood and brass, otherwise get a cheap aluminum one. When working with uneven materials such as green wood or stone, the level is used as a guide only.

TOOLS FOR WORKING WITH WOOD

Jigsaw

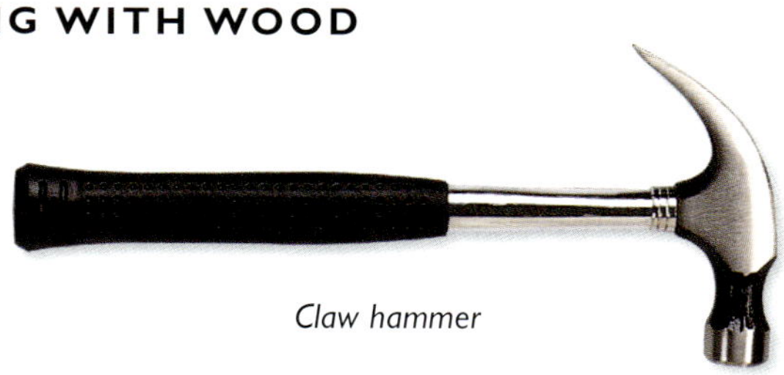

Claw hammer

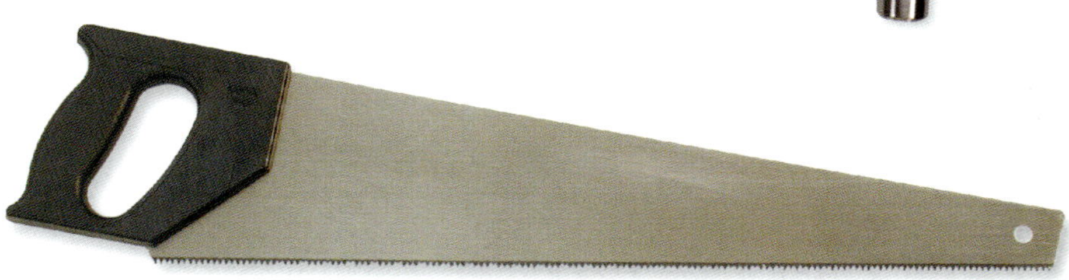

Crosscut saw

Electric drill

Drill bit for wood and metal

Flat bit

Cross-point screwdriver

Cordless drill/driver

Mallet

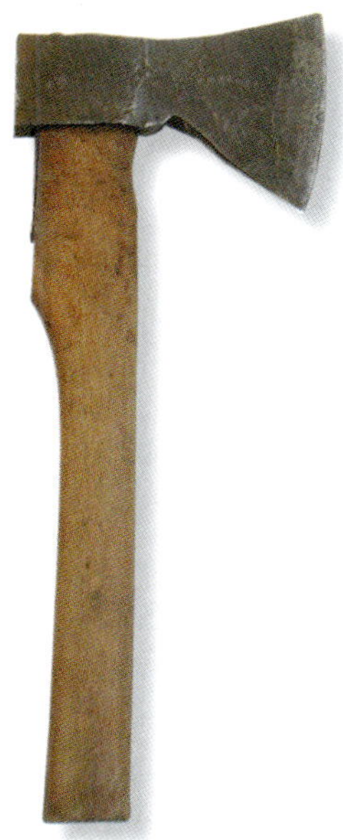
Axe

Clamp

Sawing to size

Assuming that you have purchased all your wood ready-sawn to the desired width and thickness, all you need is a top-quality, hard-toothed, crosscut saw (designed to cut across the run of the grain). In fact, most modern saws can cope with cutting both across and down the grain. It is best to buy a new, razor-sharp saw for the project, and treat it as fairly disposable. At the end of a day's work, wipe the saw with white spirit and rub it down with oil.

Sawing curves

We use an electric jigsaw for cutting decorative curves. It is a very efficient tool, easily capable of cutting wood up to 30 mm thick. A variety of blades can be fitted to suit different types of wood. To use it, set the blade close to the cutting mark (with the bed of the tool resting flat on the wood), switch on the power and then slowly advance the tool to cut slightly to the waste side of the drawn line. When you have made the cut, switch it off, wait until the blade has come to a standstill and then lift the tool clear.

CAUTION

For tricky fixing situations where the workpiece is too big, heavy, or awkward to hold (such as a large decking frame), it is safer and easier to use a clamp to hold the components securely while you work.

Making joints

The projects generally use butt joints or overlapping joints, with one piece of wood simply set close to another. But in one or two cases, half-lap joints are required. To make these, you saw halfway through the thickness of the wood, and use the axe and mallet to chop out the waste wood along the run of the grain.

Screwing, nailing and bolting

Screws, nails or bolts are generally used for joining wood to make frames. An electric drill is required for making pilot holes for screws and bolts, and a variable-speed cordless drill fitted with a cross-point screwdriver bit for driving in screws. Occasionally, we use a hand screwdriver. In most cases, screwholes don't need to be countersunk: the wood is so soft that the screwhead will cut its own countersink. When it comes to nailing, we sometimes drill pilot holes, but mostly we simply drive the nail home with the claw hammer. When tightening up bolts, much will depend upon the design of your chosen bolts. We use one or other of our garage wrenches.

TOOLS FOR BRICKWORK AND STONEWORK

Mason's hammer

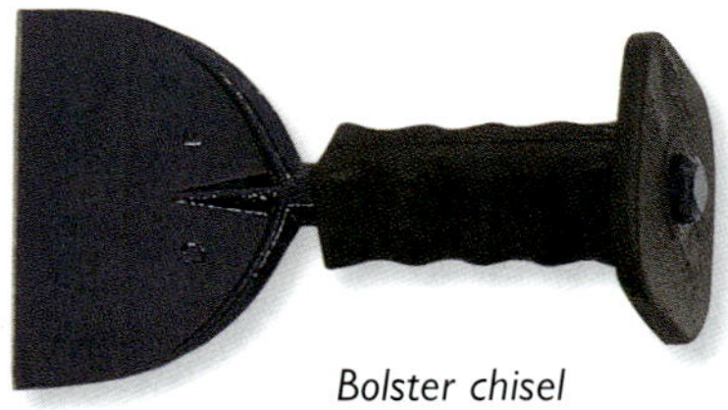

Bolster chisel

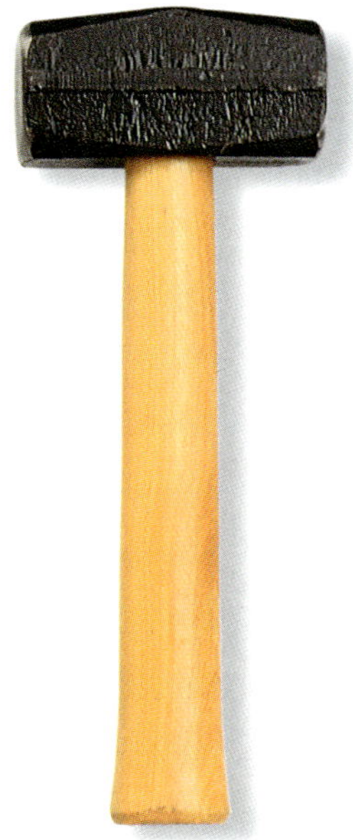

Club hammer

Angle grinder

Bricklayer's trowel

Pointing trowel

Cutting brick

Generally, it is best to avoid cutting bricks if possible. However, when the need arises, use a club hammer and bolster chisel for making precise cuts, and a mason's hammer for nibbling back a damaged edge. (A mason's hammer can also be used for removing mortar from salvaged bricks.) It is possible to use the edge of a bricklayer's trowel to chop a brick in half, but it is best to use a bolster chisel and hammer until you are more experienced. To cut a brick with a bolster chisel, set the brick on a block of wood, position the bolster chisel on the mark, and give the chisel a single, well-placed blow with the club hammer. Ideally, practise on a pile of old bricks before you start on those for your project.

Cutting stone

You need four tools for cutting stone: an angle grinder, a club hammer, a mason's hammer and a bolster chisel. To make a precise cut – to break a slab of natural or reconstituted stone – start by repeatedly running the angle grinder disc along the drawn line (on both sides of the stone) until you have a groove. Then position the stone on a wooden block, set the bolster chisel in the groove and give it a series of small taps until it breaks along the line. To trim a stone or to cut a jagged edge back to a straight line, set the stone on the ground with the edge to be worked on the far side, and use the chisel end of the mason's hammer to peck away the edge of the stone. Place the cut edge so that it is hidden from view.

CAUTION

Cutting brick and stone is potentially very dangerous – eyes, lungs, hands and feet are all susceptible. You must protect yourself by wearing a dust-mask, a pair of safety goggles, gloves and stout work boots.

Working with mortar

Working with mortar is great fun. We use a large bricklayer's trowel and a smaller pointing trowel. Once the mortar has been roughly mixed, it needs to be turned and mixed with the large trowel until it feels smooth like butter, and slices to show a firm, moist face. We use the large trowel for spreading mortar on the foundation in readiness for bedding bricks and stone, and the small trowel for buttering the ends of bricks with mortar and for pointing (see page 23). The large trowel is used with a scooping action (the mortar sitting on the back of the blade), while the small trowel is used with a spreading action, like a spatula.

When using mortar, the order of work is to spread it with the bricklayer's trowel, bed the brick or stone in it, then slice off the excess mortar. As you work, use the spirit level to test the levels of the bricks or stones. If the mortar is runny, it is too wet and you need to add a small amount of cement to the mix; if it is too crumbly, you need to add a little water followed by a sprinkling of cement.

OTHER ESSENTIAL TOOLS

Gloves

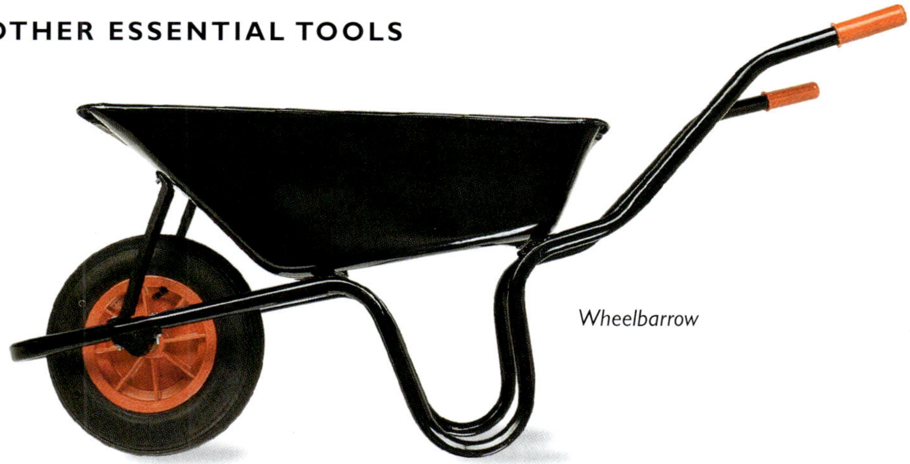

Wheelbarrow

Spade

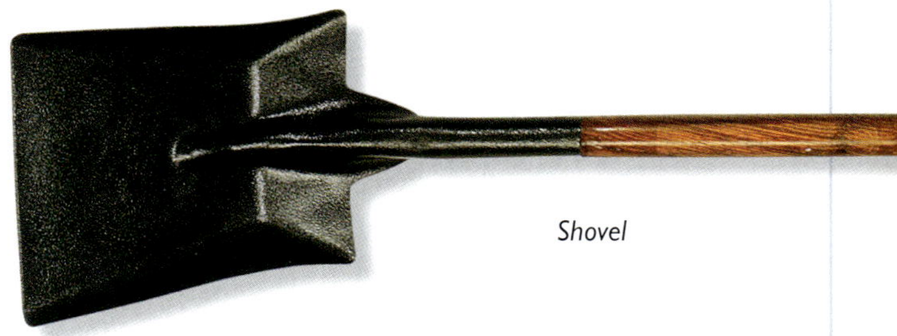

Shovel

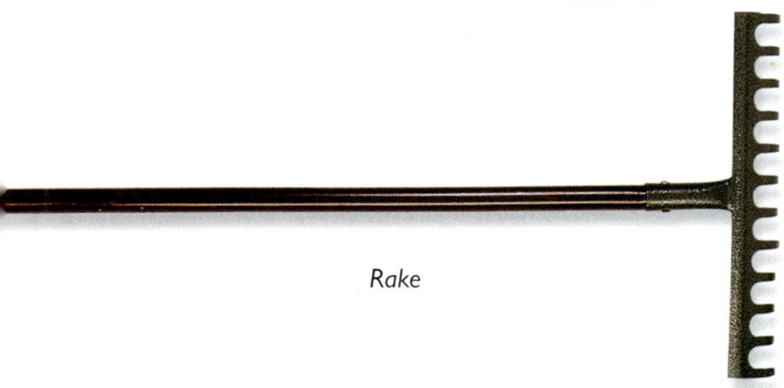

Rake

Sledgehammer

Scissors

Craft knife

Wire snips

Wrench

Starting, fixing and finishing

Where a project involves clearing a site, digging holes, mixing concrete and generally moving earth, sand and cement, a wheelbarrow is essential. A good wheelbarrow will not only save your back from a huge amount of stress and strain, but it will also allow you to move massive stones that are too heavy to lift. The best wheelbarrows have a large, inflated rubber tyre and a tip bar at the front, making it very easy to bounce your way over different levels in the garden, and just as easily come to a halt and tip out the load on the required spot.

A spade, shovel, garden rake, sledgehammer and a good pair of leather gloves are also indispensible. Always choose tools that match your strength and height – trying to move earth and sand with a shovel that is too short, or banging in a post with a sledgehammer that is too heavy, will cause you unnecessary stress and strain. If, when you are digging a hole or shovelling sand, you find that your hips or back ache, the chances are that the spade or shovel handle is too short. To help with large-scale projects that require earth to be moved, consider hiring in machinery, for example a digger or earth-compacting machine.

Alongside the heavy tools, you will also need a pair of scissors for cutting plastic sheet, a pair of wire snips, a craft knife and a wrench. It is preferable to buy new tools and keep them to be used exclusively in the garden. This is because it is not a good idea to use scissors that may have come into contact with soil, possibly near drains, in the house – especially in the kitchen or nursery.

Materials

Building materials offer so much promise, excitement and challenge! A disparate heap of materials – stone, sand, cement, wood, bricks – can be transformed, after a few days of great fun and endeavour, into a dynamic creation such as a path, patio or flight of steps, which could enhance your garden for years to come.

WOOD AND WOODEN MATERIALS

75 mm x 75 mm

150 mm x 20 mm

50 mm x 32 mm

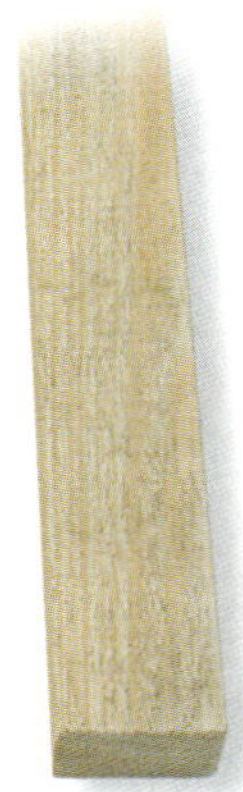

30 mm x 20 mm

90 mm x 40 mm

75 mm x 20 mm

Green wood post with bark

Skinned green wood post

Specially grooved wood

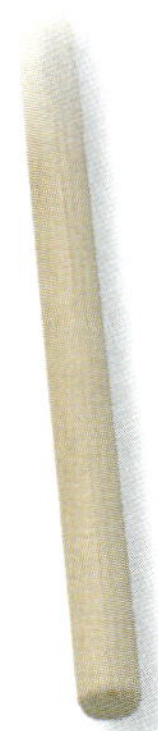

Dowel

Log roll border edging

Ball

Bark chippings

Railway sleeper

Wood stepping stone

DIY decking tile

Sawn timber section

When you visit a sawmill, you will discover that there are a number of sawn timber sections available, such as 75 mm square-section posts, or boards 150 mm wide and 20 mm thick, all sold in lengths ranging from 2 m through to 5 m. The wood is generally supplied in three ways: untreated and ready for painting, brush-treated with a brown preservative, and pressure-treated with a clear or greenish preservative.

Visit various suppliers to see what they have to offer, and to compare quality and price. Though a project might specify 2 m lengths, you may be able to cut costs by buying 4 m lengths, or 1 m lengths. Be flexible, and prepared to modify the design.

Green wood

Green wood is defined as freshly cut wood that is still wet or "green", as opposed to dry or seasoned wood. It can be purchased with or without bark, in its round, natural state, or as rough-sawn wood. Traditionally, it is worked with tools such as the saw, axe and drawknife. Green wood is ideally suited to garden projects for three good reasons. It is cheap, it instantly blends in and looks at home, and it is easy to work.

Decking and decking tiles

Decking can consist of anything from rough-sawn, part-seasoned wood straight from the sawmill, to fully seasoned wood that has been planed and treated with preservative. In fact, decking can be just about any wood that you choose to use. Decking tiles, on the other hand, are specially designed for the purpose. Such tiles are usually between 300 mm and 500 mm square and can easily be made up from a number of identical thin sections that have been planed and pre-treated with preservative. All you do is arrange the sections to make a square duck board or tile – seven on top and three on the underside – and fix them with nails or screws.

Bark chippings

Bark chippings consist of tree bark that has been ground up to a uniform size. It looks good spread on a path, or surrounding decking tiles, and when it eventually breaks down, you can spread it over the flowerbeds as a mulch.

Other useful materials

The projects use railway sleepers, log roll border edging (half-round sections fixed to wire), slices cut from the trunk of a tree, and rough wooden balls sold as fence post finials. These materials can be purchased from fence-makers, sawmills and garden centres. When buying railway sleepers, try to search out some that are free from great blobs of grease and tar, and be ready to haggle over the price. We found huge differences in price between suppliers, with the most expensive from garden centres and the cheapest from companies specializing in salvage and demolition.

BUYING TIPS

- Ferret out the best prices. Phone around, ask for quotes and then go to look at the products. Small shops are usually the most expensive, followed by garden centres, builders' merchants and specialist dealers.
- Be flexible when it comes to sizes, and ready to change the shape and size of the project to suit available materials.
- Never buy anything unseen. Never let the delivery man unload without first checking the load. Always obtain a receipt.
- Try to buy in bulk whenever possible.
- If you can persuade one of your friends or neighbours to build a project too, you can both lower your costs by buying bulk orders of materials that you have in common.

WOOD FIXINGS

Countersunk cross-headed decking screw

Bright steel flat-headed nail

Galvanized fence staple

Zinc-plated, countersunk cross-headed woodscrew

Zinc-plated coach bolt, washer and nut

Across the range of projects we have used countersunk, cross-headed decking screws, zinc-plated, countersunk cross-headed screws, steel nails, galvanized staples, and zinc-plated coach bolts with washers and nuts to fit. Wood fixings can be purchased in small packs, but it is much cheaper to buy them by weight (and it's always cheaper to buy them in bulk from a specialist supplier). You might only want a small quantity, but they aren't perishable, so why not buy more than you need and keep them for future use.

For interior woodwork we always use slot-headed screws (in situations where we are driving in a few of them by hand with a screwdriver), but when we are building garden structures that require lots of screws, we always opt for cross-headed screws used in conjunction with a cordless screwdriver. Cross-headed screws are designed to be driven in with a power screwdriver – they go in more readily than slot-headed screws and the process is easier than screwing in by hand.

BRICK AND STONE MATERIALS

Brick

Ceramic tile

Limestone block

York stone

Reconstituted stone square paver

Reconstituted stone radius tile paver

Reconstituted stone paver for circular patio

Reconstituted stone block for building walls

Rope-top edging in reconstituted stone

Ceramic border edging

Patio section made from reconstituted stone setts

Reconstituted stone corner post

Cobbles

Yellow sand

Smooth gravel

Ornamental gravel

Bricks and tiles

Bricks and tiles are made from kiln-fired clay. The colours range from red-browns through to greeny blues, with all manner of subtle mixes and tints in between. Their textures vary from gritty and rough to glazed and shiny, and they look perfect in the garden.

Reconstituted stone

Reconstituted stone blocks and slabs are made from concrete with an aggregate containing the stone that they seek to imitate. Many reconstituted slabs look so convincing that they cannot easily be distinguished from the real thing. The stone comes in all sorts of shapes, sizes, colours and textures – tessellating shapes that look like red quarry tiles, sandstone paving slabs, on-edge tiles, sandstone flagstones, ceramic rope-topped edging tiles, slabs made to look old and worn, and many other forms and designs. If you want to cut costs, reconstituted stone is a great idea.

Natural stone

The best types of stone to use in the garden are limestone, sandstone and granite. Smooth, white limestone boulders are perfect as a feature edging. Sandstone, ranging in colour from pinky-brown to blackish green, is a good choice for dry-stone walling, stepping stones and flagstones. Granite offers a selection of interesting colours, from dark green-blue through to a pinkish grey. If possible, search out salvaged pieces. You could use salvaged road setts to edge a paving circle, or pieces of quarry stone as feature stones to edge a flight of steps, and so on.

Sand and gravel

Soft sand, sometimes called builder's sand, is used for making mortar, while sharp sand is used for concrete. Locally produced sand always complements the colour of the stone and brick in the area. Be wary about buying bagged sand from a distant quarry, as it will be a different colour to your local stone. Gravel comes in many grades, from fine pea gravel to gravel the size of a small egg. Both gravel and sand are best purchased in bulk from a local pit.

BUYING TIPS

- Make sure that sand has been washed and screened so that it doesn't contain any salt, clay, animal or vegetable matter. Salty sand will kill your plants, weaken mortar and concrete mixes, and effervesce out of stonework and brickwork. Clay will weaken mortar and concrete mixes.
- A lorry-load of sand will always work out much cheaper than bagged sand, sometimes a quarter of the cost. The next cheapest option is to have the sand delivered by the tonne in a huge bag. The supplier will use a crane to unload the bag.
- If you decide to go and collect pre-bagged sand in your car, be aware of the consequences. The dead weight will alter your steering and braking, and might well damage your springs.
- Meet the delivery lorry when it arrives with your order of sand and gravel, just in case the order is incorrect or the driver attempts to unload it in the wrong place.

CONCRETE AND MORTAR

How to mix concrete

A good mix for concrete consists of 1 part cement, 2 parts sharp sand and 3 parts aggregate. The ingredients can be measured with a shovel or bucket. Put the sand on a board or in a wheelbarrow, followed by the cement powder. Turn over the mixture with the shovel until well blended, and heap up. Dig a hole in the centre, pour in a small amount of water, and gradually drag the mixture into the water. When all the cement has been mixed in, add the aggregate, followed by more water. Continue mixing, all the while adding water and turning over the heap, until you achieve a mixture that will hold its shape when formed into a ridge.

Sharp sand

Sand and gravel

Cement

How to mix mortar

To make mortar, use 1 part cement and 3 parts soft sand. Put the sand on a board or in a wheelbarrow, followed by the cement powder. Use a shovel to mix the ingredients until they are well blended, then form into a heap. Dig a hole in the centre and pour in a small quantity of water. Gradually drag the dry ingredients into the water. Continue adding water and turning the heap until you achieve a mortar with a firm, buttery consistency. A slice of mortar should stand up without crumbling. A good test is to take a dampened brick and butter one face with the mortar: it should stick and hold its shape without running.

OTHER USEFUL MATERIALS

Chicken wire makes a great anti-slip surface – buy the smallest size of mesh. Black plastic sheeting is good for holding back the growth of weeds. You can either buy the very expensive woven sheet that is specifically designed to allow water to drain away, or you can simply go for the cheapest plastic that you can find, and punch it full of holes. If the sheeting is going to go under gravel or bark, you can use just about any plastic that comes to hand, such as plastic bags, old packaging or woven plastic sacks.

Foundations

Just about every path, step and patio starts with a foundation. But if you are under the impression that every foundation needs to be a massive concrete slab, that is not the case. There are many options, ranging from gravel to crushed stone, compacted hardcore or concrete. This section tells you how to select a suitable foundation.

PATIO AND PATH FOUNDATIONS

Once you have decided on the path or patio, you need to study the site. Dig a small hole and have a good look at the ground under the topsoil. Is it hard or soft? Is there a lot of rock and rubble, or is there a layer of clay or sand? Is it wet or dry? Does water soak away swiftly, or does it sit in a puddle? Well-drained, compacted soil needs less of a foundation than more unstable areas. The options for a foundation range from a trench filled with gravel to a trench packed with compacted hardcore and topped by a layer of concrete (and various combinations in between), so in the light of your survey, spend time considering your needs.

For example, when we built the Snake-pattern Cobble Path (see page 108), we found that the site was so wet and boggy that we needed to lay a concrete slab. The planned site for the Decking Tile Patio (see page 34) was covered by such a thick layer of bark chippings that we only needed the lightest of foundations – just enough to spread the load from the weight of the patio.

If the site is dry, rocky and stable, you can get away with a thin layer of hardcore and not much else. But if the site is wet, squashy and unstable, you need to dig a trench, half-fill it with gravel for drainage, and then top it off with a generous layer of concrete. Think hard about your expectations for the project. Do you want it to last for twenty years, or are you happy for it to crumble back into the landscape after a few years? If you want it to be permanent and unshakable, a concrete slab is the answer. But if you only want it to last for a few years and don't really mind if it moves with the passing of the seasons, a layer of well-compacted hardcore will do the trick. Consider the options, think hard about the time, costs and energy required, and then make your decision.

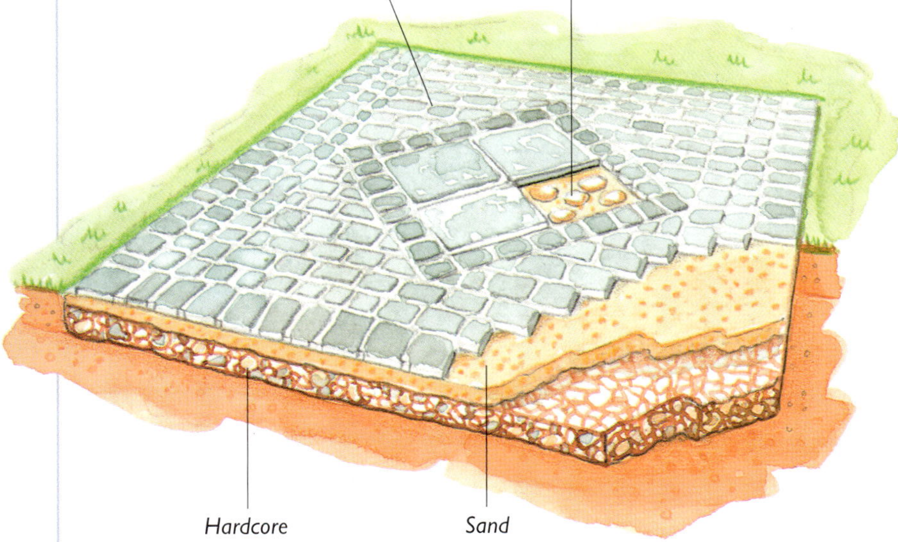

ABOVE A decorative patio made of reconstituted stone slabs set on a foundation of compacted sand spread over hardcore. This foundation is suitable for use on well-drained, compacted soil.

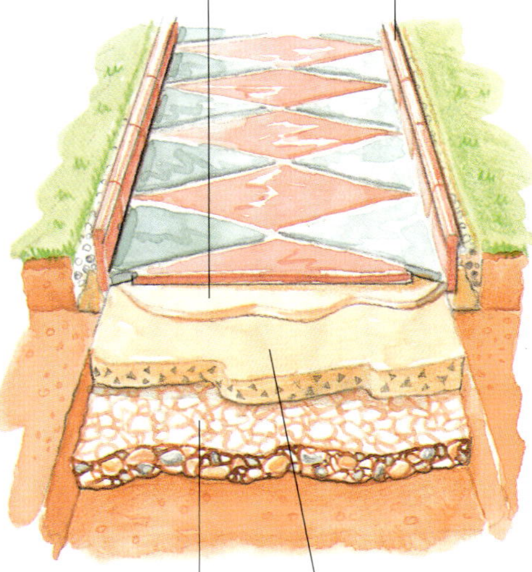

ABOVE For a path that will get a lot of use, slabs are set on a foundation of hardcore topped with concrete, and bedded on a thin layer of mortar.

FOUNDATIONS FOR STEPS

All steps need some sort of foundation, even if it is only a couple of concrete blocks (as with the Wooden Stairway on page 120). Under a short flight of railway sleeper steps, you can get away with a foundation of just a layer of hardcore because it doesn't matter too much if the steps move independently of each other. Stone steps definitely need a stable foundation that is going to stay put, and must be built on concrete. If we are constructing stone steps up a firm slope (stony ground with plenty of drainage), we start by building an extra-large foundation slab under the bottom step, which becomes the anchor for the rest of the flight of steps. First, we clear the ground under the first and second steps, put in the hardcore, and then lay a concrete slab that runs back into the slope. We then build up a retaining wall for the first riser, back-fill behind the riser with more hardcore, and lay a thinner concrete slab in readiness for the next riser. In this way, we gradually work up the slope building the other steps.

The guiding rule to follow is the wetter the ground, the more hardcore and the thicker the layer of concrete required for the foundation. The best way to proceed is to look at the ground, dig a small trial hole, and then take it from there.

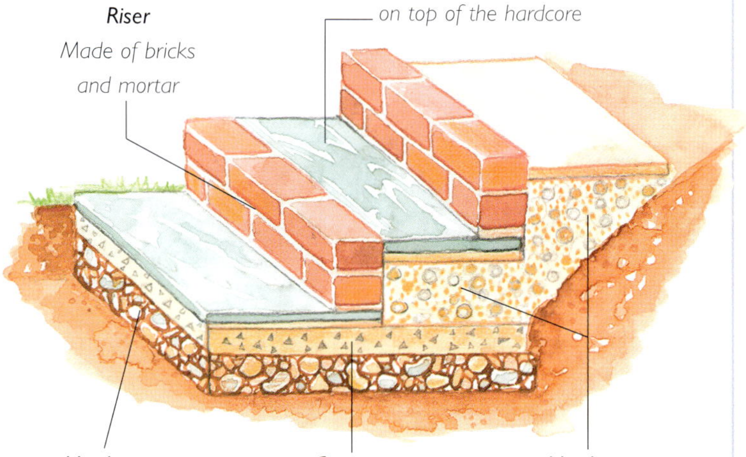

ABOVE Steps that will get a lot of traffic require a sturdy foundation of hardcore and concrete built in stages from the bottom step upwards. The most important part of the foundation is under the lowest step.

MAKING A FOUNDATION SLAB

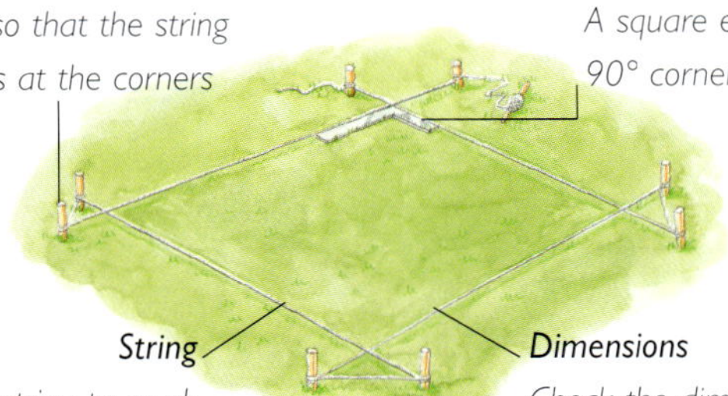

ABOVE Pegs, string and a tape measure (a square may also be useful) are used to mark out a rectangular area of the correct size.

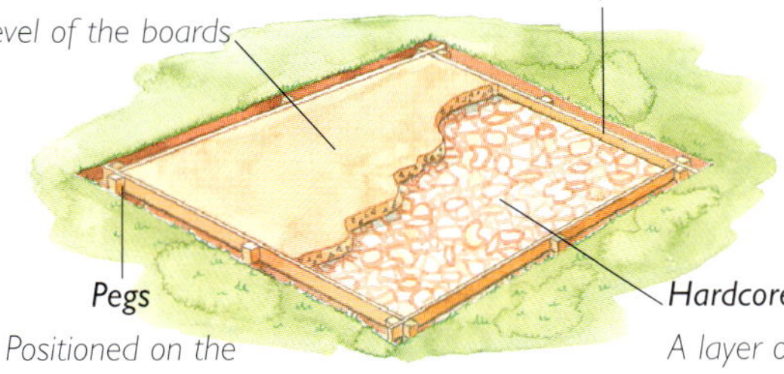

ABOVE A frame made from boards and pegs – called formwork – is used for casting a concrete foundation slab.

Every project will need a slightly different type of foundation slab, according to the configuration of the formwork and the proportions of hardcore to concrete required to suit the weight of the project and the type of site. The basic procedure is given below.

Procedure for making a foundation slab

1 Use a tape measure, string and wooden pegs to mark the outer limits of the foundation (the overall size of the slab, plus the thickness of the formwork boards, plus 100 mm all round). For example, if you want a finished concrete slab 2 m square, and the formwork boards are 20 mm thick, you need to set out a 2.24 m square. Put two pegs at each corner, so that the string line runs around the site without a break. If the foundation is rectilinear, use a square to ensure that the corners are at right angles.

2 Slice back the turf and dig down to a depth of about 200 mm. Level the base. Remove all the earth and turf from the site. Spread a 100 mm layer of hardcore over the whole site, and stamp it flat with the sledgehammer. Make sure that the hardcore is well compacted, with no cavities or loose areas. Pay particular attention to the edges. Build the formwork using square wooden pegs and 100 mm-wide boards. Use screws rather than nails to fix the boards to the pegs, to avoid knocking the pegs askew. Use a spirit level to ensure that the tops of the boards are level.

3 Mix the concrete: 1 part cement, 2 parts sharp sand and 3 parts aggregate. Pour it into the formwork and use a wooden batten to tamp it level with the top of the formwork. If the weather is hot, repeatedly spray a fine mist of water over the concrete to ensure a long curing time. If rain threatens, cover the slab with a tarpaulin.

Brickwork and stonework techniques

In many ways, the art and craft of good brickwork and stonework can be likened to building a very complex piece of Japanese woodwork. The trick is to fit the components together with the minimum of measuring and as few cuts as possible. If you do have to make a cut, the challenge is to get it right the first time around!

WORKING WITH BRICK AND STONE

A good deal of the enjoyment of working with brick and stone is derived from studying the forms and working out how best to fit them together. If you can use the various bricks and stones as you find them – they might be new, salvaged, seconds or left over from another job – so much the better. If cutting the materials is unavoidable, study the bricks and stones to work out how they can be fitted with the minimum of cuts. Always opt for straight cuts rather than attempting intricate curves.

CUTTING BRICK AND STONE

Cutting brick and stone

Brick and stone can be cut with a traditional bolster chisel and club hammer, in which case the procedure is relatively slow and quiet, but the break is not very reliable. Alternatively, you can go for the noisy, but more certain, option of using an angle grinder.

The traditional way of cutting bricks is to hold the brick in your hand and give it a couple of hard chops with a bricklayer's trowel. But if you are a beginner, use a bolster chisel. Position the brick on a firm surface, set the bolster chisel on the marked line, and give it a well-placed blow with the club hammer. Natural and reconstituted stone can be cut in much the same way. However, the easiest method is to first score the line with the angle grinder and then use the chisel to make the final cut.

CAUTION

Stone-cutting is potentially very dangerous, with lots of dust and sharp splinters, so wear a dust-mask, goggles, ear defenders, strong gloves and stout boots.

Procedure for cutting stone

1 Set the slab flat on the grass and use a tape measure, chalk and straight-edge to draw the line of cut. Brace your body, hold the angle grinder so that the wheel is at right angles to the slab, and switch on the power. Set the spinning disc on the chalk line and make a light, scoring cut. Make several runs to deepen the cut, then switch off the power, flip the slab over, and repeat the whole procedure on the other side.

2 Take the bolster chisel in one hand and the club hammer in the other, and set the edge of the chisel into the scored channel. Tap the chisel with a series of light passes, gradually increasing the power of the blows. Concentrate on the centre area, rather than the edges. Continue until the stone breaks into two.

ABOVE Use an angle grinder to score a deep line on both faces of the paver. Hold the grinder firmly and keep your feet out of the way.
BELOW Complete the cut by breaking the stone in two using a bolster chisel and hammer.

LAYING PAVING SLABS

ABOVE Set the slab on five blobs of mortar – one at each corner and one in the middle. Tap the slab level and do not stand on it until dry.

Start by laying a foundation. If the ground is stony and well drained, hardcore topped with sand is adequate. If the ground is wet and badly drained, you need a foundation of gravel covered with hardcore, topped off with concrete.

Once the foundation is in place, have a trial run and set out the slabs without mortar. See how they fit together, check how many are required and whether or not you need to cut any of them. When you are happy with the arrangement, mix a pile of stiff mortar. Dampen the underside of a slab, set five generous daubs of mortar on the foundation and gently bed the slab into position. Make adjustments by tapping the slab with the handle of a club hammer, and check the level with a spirit level.

POINTING WITH MORTAR

ABOVE The joints between bricks need to be filled neatly with mortar. Use the edge of the trowel to wipe the mortar into the joint. Approach from both sides in order to create a peaked effect.

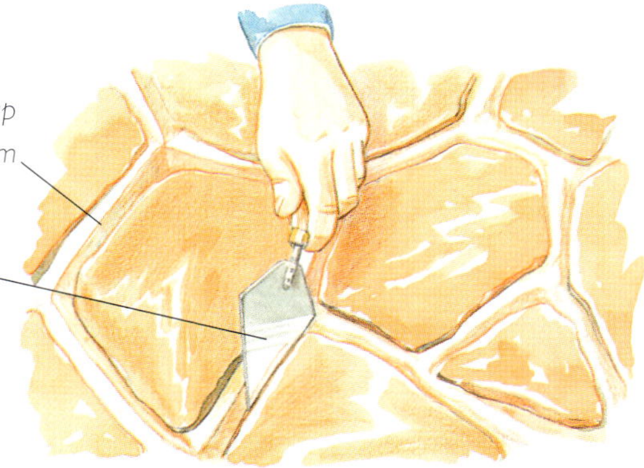

ABOVE When positioning crazy paving that will have the gaps filled with wet mortar, leave a minimum gap of 10 mm between each stone and preferably more (otherwise it is difficult to fill the gaps).

When you have set your bricks or stone slabs in place to make a wall, the gaps between them, or joints, need to be filled or pointed with mortar. To fill brickwork, start by using the tip of the pointing trowel to tidy up the joints as they stand. Then use the pointing trowel to spread a generous slice of fresh mortar on the face of the bricklayer's trowel. Spread the mortar until it is more or less the same thickness as the joint that you want to fill. Using the edge of the pointing trowel like a spatula, lift the mortar clear with a slicing, wiping action, so that it finishes up on the back edge of the trowel. This movement is tricky, so you will need to practise to get it right. Push the slice of mortar into the gap with a firm, wiping action. Repeat this procedure on all the joints to be filled. Finally, wash the trowel in clean water, then tidy up the vertical and horizontal joints.

Filling a paved area is done in much the same way – the only difference is that you have to adjust the thickness of the mortar on the bricklayer's trowel, and angle your approach to suit the width and position of the joint to be filled.

GAP-FILLING PAVING SLABS WITH DRY MORTAR OR SAND

Brush the slabs to remove any stray blobs of mortar, then leave them until the mortar underneath has set and the slabs are completely dry. It's important that the paving is absolutely dry. You also need to undertake the task on a fine, sunny day, not when the weather is damp and overcast. Decide whether to fill the joints with sand or dry-mix mortar. If you decide on sand, search around for fine silver sand. The sand needs to be bone dry. If you want to use dry-mix mortar, mix a small heap in the proportions of 1 part cement to 3 parts fine sand. Once again, it important that all the ingredients are dry. Make sure that the mixture does not contain any stones, hard lumps or other debris.

Heap the sand or dry-mix mortar on the paving and use a soft-bristled broom to gently ease it into the joints. Run the brush in all directions until all the joints have been filled. Make sure that the surface of the slabs is free from dry-mix mortar. Wait until the day after it first rains before walking on the paving.

Woodwork techniques

Woodwork is an exciting, calming and therapeutic activity, and for the projects in this book, you can enjoy working outside in spring and summer. Later, you can revel in showing off the completed project to your friends and family, and get pleasure from seeing how it enriches the garden. The following techniques will enable you to complete all the projects with the minimum of expertise, effort and expense.

WORKING WITH WOOD

Don't worry if you are a raw beginner. Do not be intimidated by visions of highly finished, traditional woodwork – garden woodwork is much easier to do and altogether less hidebound, with no complex jointing procedures or necessity to plane with the grain. Of course garden woodwork does require that you learn one or two basic techniques, but they are not difficult. If you are capable of using a saw, holding a chisel, setting a post in the ground, cutting wood to length, cutting a few basic curves, banging in nails, driving in screws, and cutting one or two joints, you are quite able to make all the projects in this book.

SETTING POSTS INTO THE GROUND

Traditionally, the below-ground section of wooden posts was charred or tarred for protection before being set in a mix of clay and rubble. Today, posts are simply purchased ready-treated with preservative, and supported in either hardcore or concrete. Start by digging a hole one spade width square and about two spade spits deep. Try to keep the hole straight-sided and as narrow as possible. If the ground is reasonably dry and well drained, set the post on a piece of old tile or brick, check with the spirit level that it is perfectly upright, and then compact hardcore around it. If the post needs a bit more support, dig the hole as already described, set the post upright on the brick or tile, with a couple of stays and a small amount of hardcore to hold it in position, then fill the hole with concrete. Leave the concrete to set overnight.

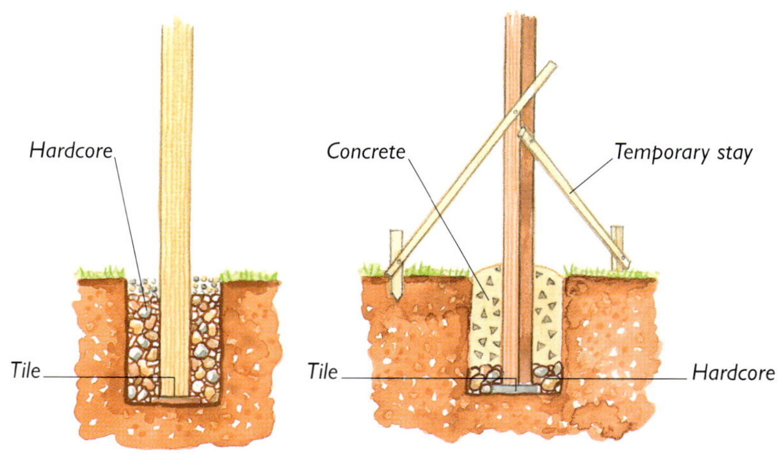

ABOVE In firm, dry soil, a post can be set in a hole and surrounded by compacted rubble. For other soil types, it is best to use concrete in addition to hardcore. Lengths of wood are used to hold the post in position until the concrete has set.

CUTTING WOOD TO LENGTH

If you have bought all your wood in prepared sections in order to make the projects to exactly the dimensions described, all you need to do is cut the wood to length with straight cuts.

To make a straight cut at right angles to the face or edge of the wood (across the run of the grain), take the set square and a carpenter's pencil, and strike a line around the wood. Let's say that you want to cut 100 mm off the end of a 75 mm-square post. Hold the wooden handle of the square (sometimes known as the "stock") hard against the workpiece, and run a pencil line against the edge of the steel blade. Repeat this procedure on all faces and edges of the post until the line encircles the wood.

This done, support the workpiece on a couple of portable workbenches, with the line of cut just clear of the bench. Take the crosscut saw and position the teeth to the waste side of the drawn line, and make a few short, dragging strokes. When the saw begins to bite, use the full length of it to make the cut. Keep sighting down the saw to ensure that the blade is running true with the drawn line. When you come to within a few strokes of finishing the cut, hook your free hand under the piece of waste, or ask a helper to do so, and make lighter strokes until the wood is sawn through. On no account let the wood break off under its own weight, as it is likely to splinter.

CUTTING CURVES IN WOOD

For cutting swift, broad curves in thick wood, we favour a power jigsaw. Bridge the workpiece across a couple of workbenches, so that the area to be cut is well clear of the benches. Set the bed of the saw on the workpiece with the blade just clear of the wood. Switch on the power and slowly advance the tool so that the line of cut runs slightly to the waste side of the drawn line. When you approach the end of the cut, ease off the pressure, advance until the blade runs clear of the wood, and then switch off the power. Keep your attention fixed on the saw until the blade comes to a standstill, and then remove the blade from the wood.

RIGHT Use a jigsaw for cutting curved shapes (but never use a jigsaw on round-section wood). Choose a blade type to suit the job.

NAILING, SCREWING AND BOLTING

ABOVE Use screws positioned diagonally to create a strong joint. Drill holes in the top piece of wood before screwing.

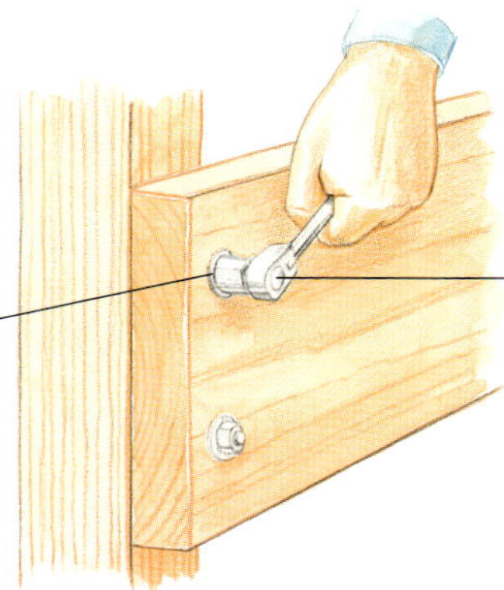

ABOVE Bolts make very strong joints, which are necessary in large frameworks such as those used to support decking boards.

The projects use three types of fixings for jointing wood: countersunk cross-headed screws, nails (bright steel and galvanized), and coach bolts with nuts and washers to fit. Using an electric drill, we drill holes for bolts and make pilot holes for screws. However, if the screw positions occur well away from the end of the wood, where there is little risk of the wood splitting, we sometimes drive in the screws without drilling pilot holes. We use a cordless electric screwdriver fitted with a cross-point bit. You could use a hand screwdriver, but the cordless screwdriver gets the job done faster, and the process is a lot less tiring. It's a wonderful tool for big projects with lots of parts that need to be screwed together. If you intend working over several days, remember to recharge the cordless drill overnight.

When extra strength is required, we use coach bolts for the primary joints. Measure the diameter of the bolt and drill a hole the same size through the workpiece. It is important that the shank of the bolt is a tight fit in the hole. Knock the bolt into place so that the square section on the underside of the domed head locks into the drilled hole. Slide a washer and nut on the bolt, and tighten up the nut with a ratchet wrench.

CUTTING JOINTS

Apart from butted and overlapping joints, when two or more components are set face to face and fixed with screws or bolts, the only other joint we use for the projects is the half-lap. This involves lapping one component over another, and then cutting half the material away from each part so that they fit together with faces and edges flush. For example, in the Green Wood Walkway (see page 56), the floor beams are lapped end to end.

The procedure is as follows. Use the tape measure, pencil and square to set out the size and shape of the half-laps, then cut down the shoulder-line with a saw. Finally, set an axe on the mark and use a mallet to chop out the waste. If you are anxious about using the axe, you could substitute a very wide chisel instead. Whatever the cutting context, the rule is to saw across the grain and split with the run of the grain.

Paths

Paths enhance the garden in the sense that they are functionally desirable – you might need a path to cross a lawn, to mark out the quickest route, or so that you won't get your feet muddy. But paths also stimulate the imagination. A path slowly winding out of sight round a corner or through a gate in a wall or hedge can be enticing, mysterious and inspirational – a route for your feet, eyes and mind to follow.

BRICK AND STONE

ABOVE A brick and paver path which has the brick edging flush with the lawn to ensure easy mowing.

ABOVE A traditional chevron brick path with contrasting edge pieces, so there is no need to cut bricks.

ABOVE A brick and paver path is versatile – it can be arranged in any pattern and direction.

Consider how your garden might benefit by having one or more paths. Would a path save wear and tear on the lawn? Would a dry, clean path help keep the house free of muddy footprints? Would it make life easier if there were paths around the vegetable plots? Or perhaps a slow, meandering path would add a touch of excitement to an otherwise dull garden?

Undoubtedly, your choice of path will to a great extent depend on your requirements and your liking for certain materials, but some paths are more suited to certain situations than others. For example, a straight brick and stone path is decorative and hard-wearing, and perfect for running directly between two points. (If you have salvaged materials, such as bricks and stones rescued from an outhouse or shed that you are pulling down, so much the better.) A zigzag brick and stone path, or a gently curved flagstone and brick path, can be employed to provide a barrier between the lawn and the flower border. Not only can you stroll along the path to admire the plants and to do the weeding, but the width of the path also prevents the grass from invading the beds. A zigzag path can be built with the minimum of planning – in fact it can be built slowly over many months or even years. You simply put down the basic module of brick and stone, and add more modules to the left and right to fit the edge of the lawn. All these paths can be built slightly lower than the level of the lawn to aid easy mowing – a really good point in their favour!

EDGINGS FOR BRICK AND STONE PATHS

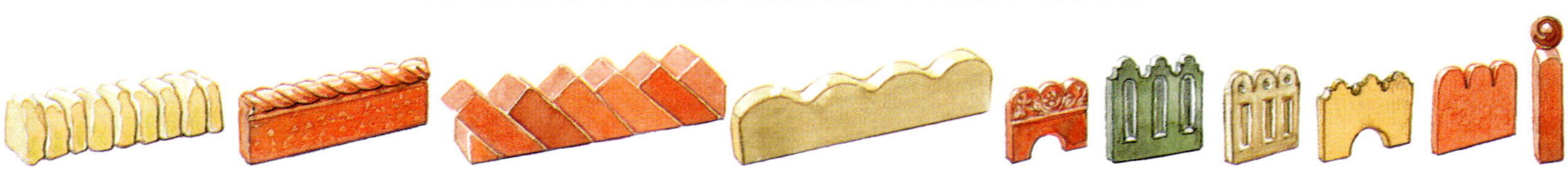

Functionally, an edging stops a path from spreading; however, it can also transform a dull path into something really dynamic. For example, you could make an edging from locally gathered fieldstone, or push in a Victorian-style ceramic rope-topped edging, or set bricks on edge to create a dog-tooth effect. The edging can be bold, or it can vanish away into the lawn to make mowing easier.

ABOVE There are many edgings to choose from: some are functional and others are purely decorative. From left to right: reconstituted stone coping block, rope-top edging, brick edging, shaped reconstituted stone block, various ceramic and reconstituted stone edging tiles and a corner post. Be aware that some edgings are so expensive that they can double the cost of a length of path.

WOODEN WALKWAYS

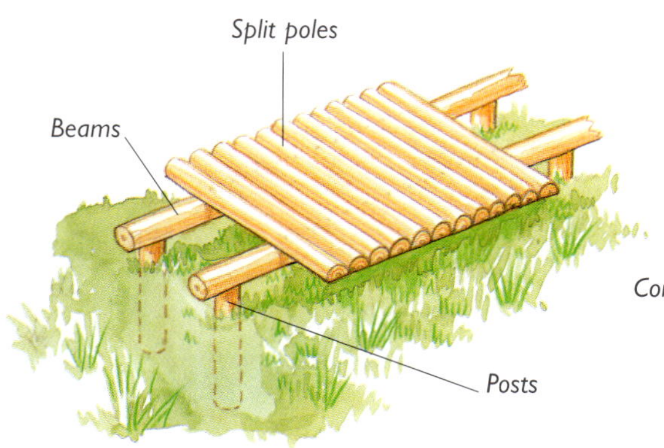

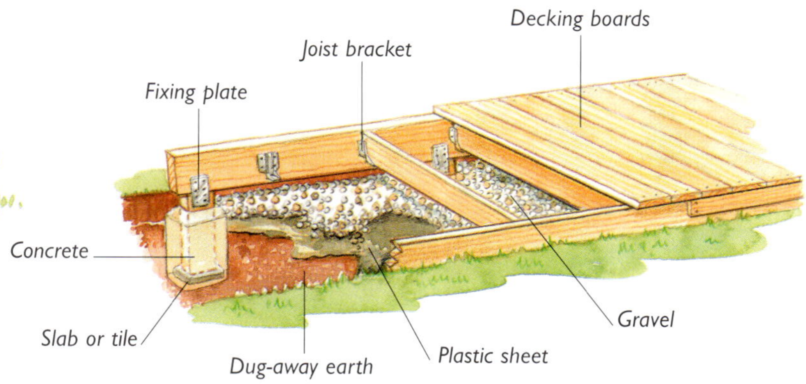

ABOVE This walkway is constructed from rustic poles with the bark removed. It has been built a little above ground level in order to minimize contact with wet grass and earth.

ABOVE A decking walkway suits more formal areas. Pressure-treated wood is used, and strong beams form the sides. If the ground is soft or wet, the supporting posts need to be set in concrete.

A wooden walkway is actually just a path or patio made of wood, which is usually slightly elevated from the ground. The structure can be made from green wood, sawn wood, or even from wood that has been planed and moulded. It may be built on a bed of gravel, on short piles (see the Green Wood Walkway on page 56), or even built on posts (see the Raised Decking on page 114). Decking originated in frontier towns in the American West, and in Australia, where wood was relatively cheap. It was often necessary to build a level surface over bumpy, wet or sloping ground, and decking provided a quick and cheap solution.

If you are considering building a wooden walkway, start by looking at your garden and studying the geography. Do you want the surface some considerable distance off the ground to accommodate an extremely sloping site? Or is it simply going to be built over slightly bumpy ground? If the ground is steeply sloped but stable, you will need long wooden posts concreted into holes, whereas if it is level but wet, you could use short stub posts set in concrete with a layer of gravel covering the ground. If the land is completely level and well drained, you can bed wooden tiles directly into gravel, without the need for posts or piles.

STEPPING-STONE PATHS

Made of natural stone, concrete slabs, bricks or wood, the good thing about stepping-stone paths is that they can be put down with the minimum of fuss and disturbance. They are also great performers when it comes to mowing the lawn – you don't have to worry about mowing around the stones, you simply ignore them. Aesthetically, stepping stones meandering across a lawn give the appearance of stony outcrops, while a path made up of sawn tree rounds, set in gravel or bark, looks beautifully at home in a wooded garden. Over time, a stepping-stone path will merge attractively into the landscape, as it gradually gets partially covered with grass, moss and fallen leaves.

Procedure for making a stepping-stone path

1 Space out the stones across your lawn. When you have achieved a good arrangement – which suits the length of your stride and complements the surrounding garden – dig around the stones with a spade and lift them to one side. Remove the turf and earth to a depth of 200 mm. Clear the turf and earth from the site.

2 Spread a 90 mm-thick layer of sand in the recess and carefully ease and bed the stone in place. Adjust the sand until the stone is level and slightly lower than the lawn. Use a hammer and a short beam of wood to wedge the stone into the underlying sand.

ABOVE These cleverly shaped decking tiles are a quick way to create a wiggly path and are an option for a well-drained modern garden.

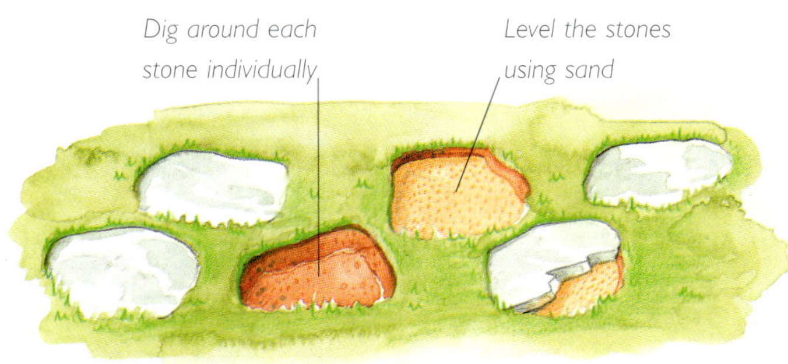

ABOVE Space natural stones to match the size of your stride. Bed the stones on a layer of sand so that they are at the same level as the grass – this will make it easy to mow the lawn.

Patios

Create a dynamic focal point in your garden by building a patio. This versatile area provides somewhere to put a table and chairs, a dry, level place for children to play, a site for the barbecue, or a spot to laze on a lounger. The options available are almost limitless – for example stone, wood, decorative combinations of materials, split-level decking or DIY kits. Make your own selection to complement the style of your garden.

BRICK AND STONE PATIOS

ABOVE A classic-style patio made from bricks and pavers in a random decorative pattern. This design allows for interspersed areas of planting, which are useful for injecting interest into large paved areas.

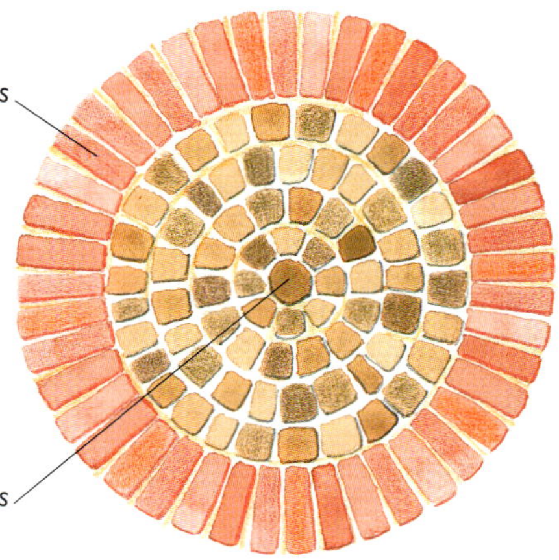

ABOVE A small, circular patio has the potential to transform a tiny garden, adding pattern and texture.

If you live in an area where the weather is damp for a good part of the year, and your garden consists of a lawn surrounded by lots of foliage, a traditional brick or stone patio will enable you to get more use out of the garden. This type of patio will last forever.

Procedure for making a brick and stone patio

1 Mark out the size of the patio with a tape measure and string. Remove all the turf and earth to a depth of about 200 mm. Rake a 100 mm layer of ballast over the bottom of the recess. Spread a thin layer of sand over the ballast and tamp it smooth with a tamping beam. Repeat this several times, until the sand is well compacted and within 70 mm of the level of the lawn.

2 Set the modules of brick and stone on generous blobs of mortar, easing them until the mortar is slightly displaced and the faces of the bricks and stones are more or less level with the lawn. Tamp the arrangement with the beam and a club hammer. Check with the spirit level and make corrections until the bricks and stones are level. Re-run this procedure for all the modules. Make sure that the various joints are staggered.

3 When all the bricks and stones are in position, leave them overnight until the mortar has set. Wait for a sunny day and then shovel a mixture of sand and grass seed over the whole patio, before using a bass broom to sweep it into all the joints. Finally, spray a thin mist of water over the patio to dampen the mixture.

EDGING FOR BRICK AND STONE PATIOS

If, when you are digging away the turf and earth for a patio, you see that the ground is wet and spongy, it would be wise to add an edging to stop the patio from spreading. You have a choice between an above-surface edging such as bricks or tiles, which will frame the whole arrangement like a picture frame, or a below-surface edging that does the job but more or less vanishes from view. Edgings can also be used purely for decorative effect.

For example, with the brick and stone patio described above, the outer bricks or stones could themselves become the edging. At the edges of the patio, replace the layers of ballast, sand and mortar with a concrete footing. In this way, the outermost bricks and stones become a containing ring, like a kerb. If you want a further edging to stand proud, dig a trench around the outermost bricks, fill with a little hardcore and bed the edging in mortar.

DECKING PATIO

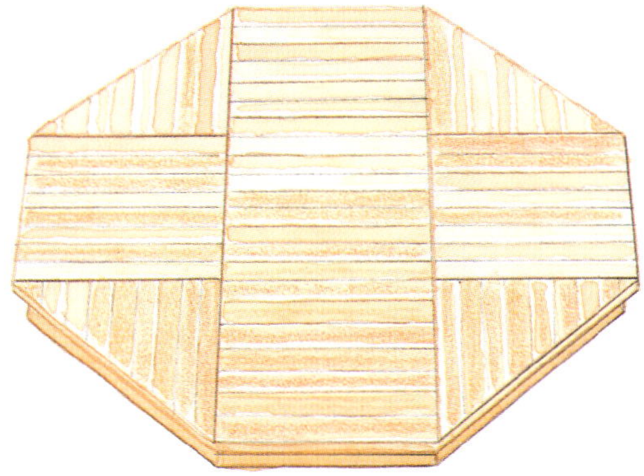

LEFT Decking patios can be shaped to suit your needs. It is not difficult to create L-shapes and angled sides (try to avoid curves).
ABOVE Decking boards can be arranged to make patterns but make sure that the ends of the decking are supported by joists beneath.

Decking patios are the perfect solution when you want to build a patio on a sloping site without going to the trouble of laying a huge foundation slab. They can be used to link the house to the garden. Decking enables you to achieve a level surface without building walls. It is rather like a massive table, with the legs of the table designed to suit the slope of the land, and steps built to run up to the level surface. This system works whatever the lay of the land, but the most dramatic results are seen if the site is really sloping, falling sharply away from the house. The structure is built in much the same way as the upper level of a house, with a framework of joists covered by a layer of boards to make a floor.

Procedure for making a patio on a sloping site

1 Use a tape measure, pegs and string to mark out the shape and size of the patio. Decide on the position of the main support posts and the spacing of the joists in relation to the shape of the patio and the thickness of the floorboards. Dig holes and set the posts in concrete. Use a tape measure and spirit level to establish the height and level of the platform. Nail temporary battens from post to post, to ensure that they remain upright.

2 Screw the outer ring of primary joists to the posts and infill with the pattern of secondary joists.

Decide how you want the floorboards to meet the outer joists. Do you want to cut the ends flush and trim them with a moulded batten? Or do you want the ends to overhang like the surface of a table? Sit down with a pencil and paper and draw out your ideas before you start cutting wood.

Run the floorboards across the joists and fix them in place with two screws for each board–joist intersection. Space the boards about 10 mm apart to allow for expansion.

DECORATIVE PATIO KITS

It is possible to buy small patios in kit form. There are circular reconstituted stone kits that look like granite stone setts, cut flagstones or bricks, kits that contain a mixture of brick and stone, circular decking kits that unroll like a carpet, and many other patterns, shapes and materials. Kits are undoubtedly a more expensive option than buying a heap of basic materials and building your own design, but they are a good choice if you want a quick, small patio with a complex pattern. One such kit comes complete with various numbered blocks and a large paper pattern. The pattern is positioned on the concrete slab, and the numbered blocks are set in place on the pattern. A dry mix of concrete and sand is then swept over the patio to fill the joints.

RIGHT These reconstituted stone setts are tesselating modules which allow various shapes and sizes of patio to be covered with circular patterns. Cobbles arranged by hand complete the design.

Steps

If you have a sloping garden, there are two ways of moving from one level to another. You can scramble up and down the slope and hope that you don't slip, or you can build one or more flights of steps. Apart from being a practical solution, steps can also function as a feature that leads the eye from one level to another.

BRICK AND STONE STEPS

ABOVE Steps with brick risers, crazy-paved treads and contrasting stone sides. The traditional soldier brick edge to the steps is an attractive detail. The crazy paving could be replaced by gravel.

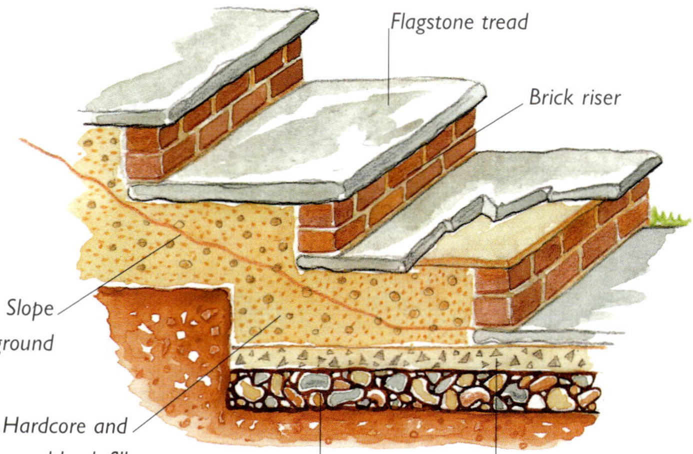

ABOVE The whole flight of steps is supported on the concrete foundation slab under the first (bottom) step. The treads are single, natural stone pavers but could be replaced with reconstituted pavers.

Garden steps can of course be made solely from brick or stone, but they are commonly made from a mix of both materials. Bricks are good for building risers and stone slabs are good for building treads, and the two forms and textures complement each other. Salvaged materials are perfect for the job. Ideally, the riser needs to be between 150–200 mm high, while the tread needs to measure between 300–400 mm from front to back.

Procedure for building steps from crazy paving and soldier bricks

1 Use a tape measure, pegs and string to establish the size and position of the steps on the ground. Lay a generous concrete slab foundation (at ground level), to run under the first riser, the first tread and second riser.

2 Build up brickwork to form the first step, making it two bricks high, with the top line made from soldier bricks set so that the heads look towards the front of the step.

3 When the mortar has cured, back-fill behind the first riser wall with compacted hardcore topped off with gravel. Lay the crazy-paving slabs on blobs of mortar to make the first tread. Check with a spirit level. Build a second riser wall off the back of the first tread, and continue as just described. Repeat the process for the whole flight of steps. If there are more than six steps, build a foundation slab for every seventh step.

USEFUL TIP

If you have trouble visualizing the finished steps, build a full-size mock-up of a single step, so that you can see how the steps are going to look in terms of size and texture.

Procedure for building brick and flagstone steps

1 Use a tape measure, pegs and string to set out the size and position of the flight of steps on the ground. Remove the turf and earth – so that you have a cut trench running up the sloping ground – and lay a concrete foundation slab at ground level to run under the first riser, the first tread and second riser.

2 Build up brickwork to form the first riser, making it two bricks high, with the best face looking towards the front of the step. Make checks with the spirit level.

3 When the mortar has cured, back-fill behind the first riser wall with compacted hardcore topped off with gravel. Butter the top of the bricks with mortar, trowel blobs of mortar on the hardcore, and set the flagstone in position with the nosing overhanging the riser wall. Check that it is level with the spirit level. Build a second riser wall off the back of the slab, and continue as already described. Repeat this procedure for the whole flight of steps.

RAILWAY SLEEPER STEPS

Salvaged railway sleepers make informal, low-rise steps which look very good in the garden. They are a handy size, measuring about 250 mm wide and 150 mm thick, relatively swift and easy to position, and virtually indestructible. (Avoid sleepers that exude tar or oil.) All you do is set the first sleeper in place and bang in posts to stop it moving forward. Next, earth is dug from the slope and compacted behind the retaining sleeper to make a level terrace, and so on up the slope. Finally, when all the sleepers are in place, you can tidy up the edge of the steps with a rockery edging, and create a tread surface with a material such as compacted stone chips.

RIGHT A design for large-scale, informal steps using railway sleepers and gravel. Arrange the sleepers as shown to make steps that are 150 mm high and as wide as you choose.

EDGINGS FOR STEPS

There are two types of step – those that are cut into a slope, and those that are freestanding. There are two common solutions to edging steps. If the steps are cut into a grass bank and made of brick, stone or railway sleepers, the bank itself can form the edging. If the steps are freestanding and made of brick or stone, the edging might be made of brick, stone or wood. For example, you could use a row of vertical logs, like a palisade. Or you could start by building brick or stone walls and then infill with the steps. You could build the flight of steps as already described in previous sections, and then build a dwarf wall off the treads. Or, easiest of all, you could pile random boulders or slabs of rough-cut stone to the side of the finished steps to make a rockery.

DECKING STEPS AND STAIRWAYS

ABOVE A simple design using very wide boards for the stringers (sides). The stringers can be bought ready-made and cut to length.
RIGHT Overlapped areas of decking can be used to form a series of broad steps or landings. The arrangement will depend on the site.

There are sometimes lots of local building regulations concerning the building of steps. If you are planning to build a flight of more than two steps, talk to the planning department and see what they recommend. There are many options: for a short flight of two treads, you can have a simple arrangement with two stringers (side boards) and treads. If the flight is higher than two treads, then for safety's sake, you also need posts and railings. If the decking is intended for family use, ideally you need a wide stairway complete with deep (front to back) and shallow (in height) steps, risers, posts and baluster rails. If you don't like the idea of a long flight of stairs running from one level to another, you can either replace the steps with a cascade of narrow decking landings, or you can break up the flight with a series of landings. To finish the wood, opt for a matt preservative rather than a high-gloss varnish.

Part 2: **Projects**

Decking tile patio

Decking tiles are a great idea. They will transform a patch of lawn or a scruffy old concrete patio into a smart, user-friendly seating area, which is perfect for entertaining or just for enjoying the sun. If you are looking for a relatively inexpensive way of creating an instant patio, decking tiles are the answer.

TIME

A single day (about six hours for all the measuring, cutting and spreading, and the rest of the time for positioning the tiles).

SPECIAL TIP

When choosing your wood, make sure that it is straight grained and free from faults. Buy wood that has been treated with preservatives.

YOU WILL NEED

Materials *for a patio 2.2 m square*

- Pine: 4 rough-sawn pieces, 2.2 m long, 75 mm square section (frame)
- Decking tiles: 160 pieces, 500 mm long, 65 mm wide and 18 mm thick.
- Dowelling: 1 piece, 300 mm long and 10 mm in diameter
- Plastic sheet: 1 piece, 2.1 m square
- Gravel: 1 bucketful of medium-sized gravel per tile
- Builder's or soft sand: 1 bucketful per tile
- Galvanized nails: 4 kg pack 36 mm long

Tools

- Pencil, ruler, tape measure and square
- Two portable workbenches
- Crosscut saw
- Axe or wide chisel
- Mallet
- Electric drill with a 10 mm flat bit
- Shovel
- Rake
- Club hammer
- Tamping beam: about 500 mm long

ALL SQUARE AND SHIPSHAPE

The wonderful thing about this project is that it can be done quickly. You don't have the problem of digging foundations – the whole idea is that you can set the decking on an existing surface without too much preparation. Whether you are going to lay the tiles on an old concrete patio, uneven crazy paving, or a squashy patch of chipped bark, you simply put down the frame, unroll the plastic, spread the gravel and sand, and lay the tiles. If you want a much larger patio, just increase the quantities accordingly.

To make a tile, cut 10 x 500 mm lengths of 65-mm wide wood and set them in position – seven on top and three underneath, and all spaced as shown – and fix them with nails.

DETAIL OF THE DECKING TILE PATIO

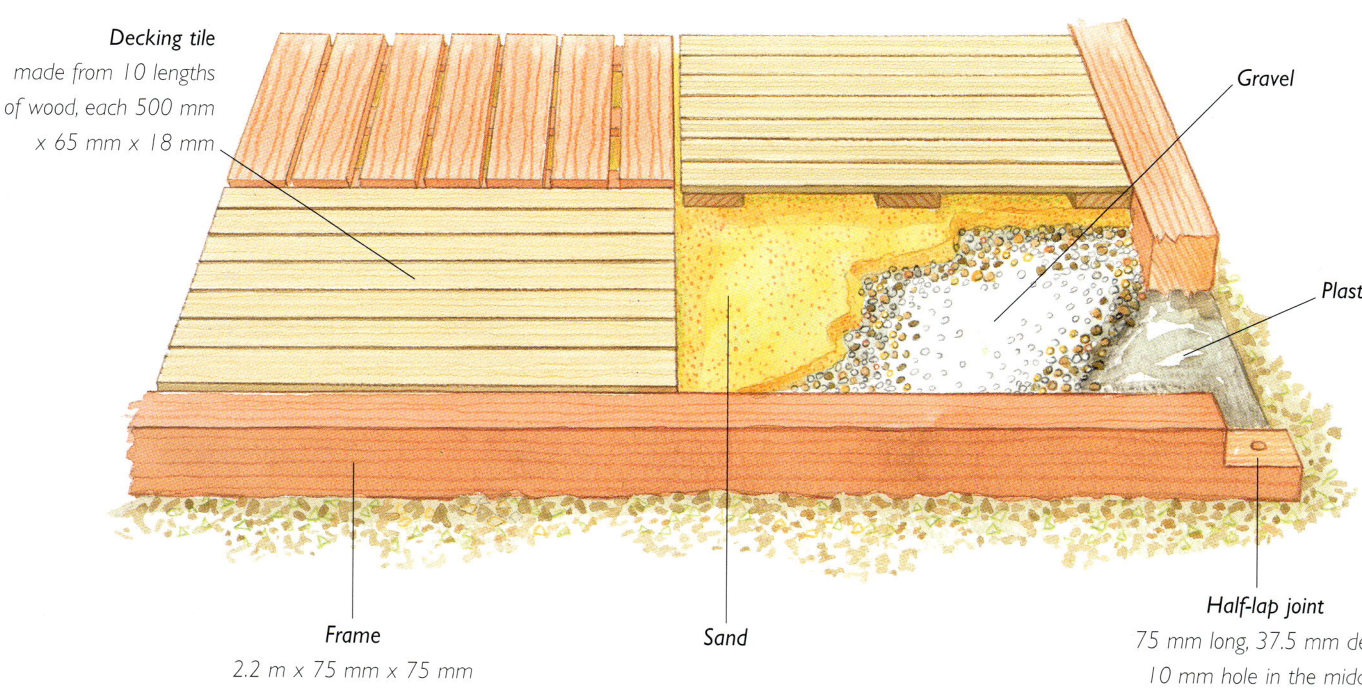

Step-by-step: **Making the decking tile patio**

Axe
Hold the axe so that the blade is square with the wood

Mallet
Give the axe a series of taps

Grain
Manoeuvre the axe so that the split runs along the grain

1 Take the four 2.2 m lengths of 75 mm square-section wood and use the tape measure, pencil and square to set out the half-laps at the ends, making them 37.5 mm deep and 75 mm long. Saw down the shoulder-line, and then use the axe and mallet to chop out the waste.

Alignment
Make sure that the two pieces of wood are at 90° to each other

2 Set the frame together, carefully squaring and aligning the half-laps. Drill through the centre of the corner joints with the 10 mm drill bit. Tap a piece of dowel, 75 mm long, through each joint.

Helpful hint

When drilling through the joint, sight down the drill so that the hole runs through the wood at right angles to the face. Ease off the pressure as the bit exits to prevent the wood from splitting.

Drainage
Spike a few holes in the plastic to allow the patio to drain freely

Plastic
Tuck the plastic sheet well under the wood

Raking
Level the gravel and cover with a layer of sand. It should reach to just below the top of the frame

3 Spread the plastic sheet over the site. Position the frame squarely on it, so that the edges of the plastic are covered. Rake a thin layer of gravel over the plastic sheet, and top it off with a layer of sand, filling the frame to just below the top.

Tamping
Tap the beam with the hammer until the tile is level with the top of the frame

4 Gently ease the tiles into position. Finally, use the club hammer and tamping beam to bed the tiles into the sand, ensuring that they are level with each other and with the frame.

Helpful hint

When ordering decking tiles, specify ones that have been treated with preservative. Avoid tiles with areas of mould, splits or other damage. Some suppliers store materials outside – if so, check that the tiles have not suffered because of it.

Zigzag brick border path

Bricks make a most attractive path, which is perfect for edging a lawn and visually blending it into the flower borders, and is sturdy enough to cope with a wheelbarrow being pushed up and down it. An added advantage of this type of path is that it allows the edge of the lawn to be mowed easily – you just ignore the path and mow over it.

TIME

One day for a 32-brick path.

SPECIAL TIP

Brick prices vary hugely. We halved our costs by using seconds, which are perfectly suitable for the task.

PERSPECTIVE VIEW OF THE ZIGZAG BRICK BORDER PATH

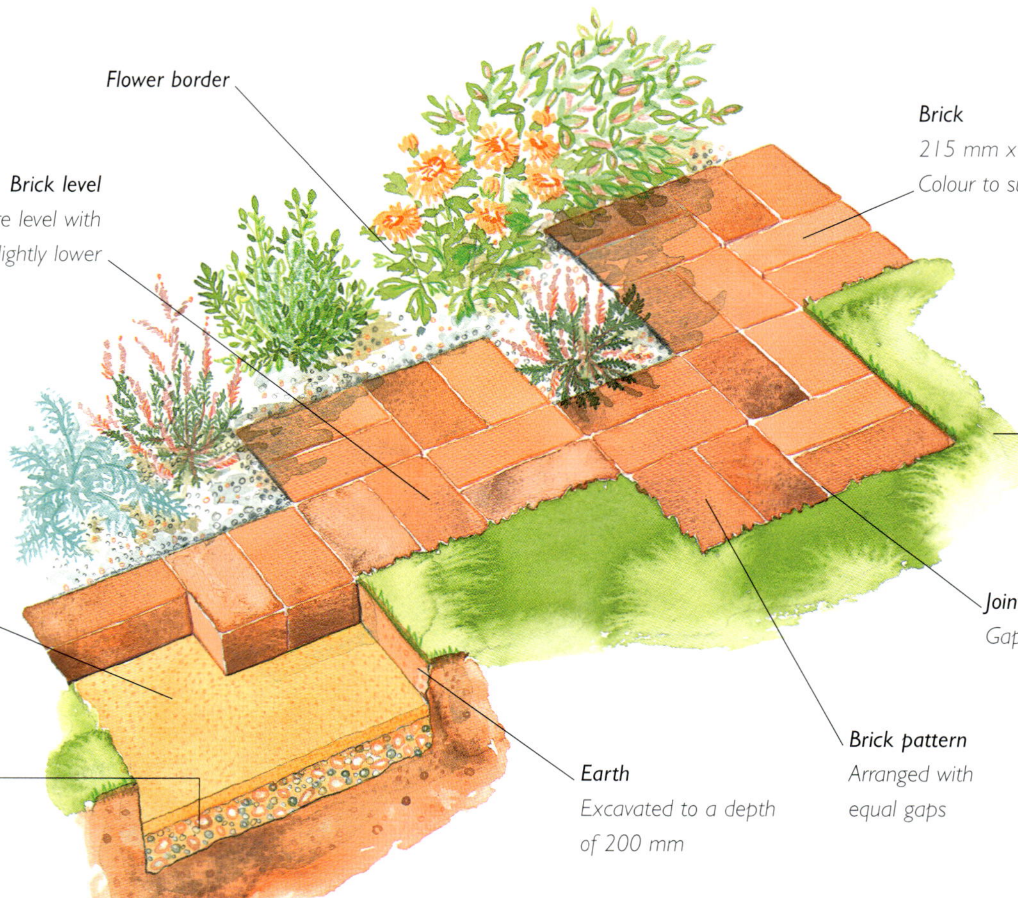

YOU WILL NEED

Materials *for a path made from 4 modules of brick pattern, 440 mm square*

- Bricks: 32 bricks, 215 mm long, 102.5 mm wide and 65 mm thick (colour and texture to suit your needs)
- Builder's or soft sand: about 1 bucketful per 8-brick square
- Ballast: about 1 bucketful per 8-brick square

Tools

- Spade
- Fork
- Wheelbarrow
- Shovel
- Rake
- Tamping beam: about 450 mm long, 20 mm thick and 100 mm wide
- Club hammer
- Brush

ZIGZAGGING ABOUT THE GARDEN

Wander round your garden and imagine how, by building zigzag brick paths, you could both tidy up the border edgings and simplify the mowing of the lawn. The design is based on a 215 mm square made of two bricks, four of which are placed together to make a larger 440 mm square. By taking this 440 mm square as the basic module, it is possible to free-flow the squares together to create the characteristic zigzag design. The great thing about this technique is that you don't have to use a tape measure – you simply set the bricks directly on the ground.

We have cut costs by using seconds, but you can also economise by using old bricks, such as those salvaged from a building site. Position the bricks with the frog or depression on the underside. Avoid bricks that show cracks or holes.

Step-by-step: **Making the zigzag brick border path**

Alignment
Sight down the row of bricks to ensure that they are in line

Design
Take time arranging the bricks to your satisfaction

Marking
Use the spade to mark around the edges of the bricks

1 Arrange the bricks so that they bleed into the flower border from the lawn. When you have achieved a pleasing design, carefully cut around the path shape with a sharp spade.

Raking
Use the head of the rake to tamp the ballast into place

Ballast
Be generous with the ballast, to avoid cavities

2 One or two modules at a time, remove the turf and earth to a depth of about 200 mm. Spread and rake a 100 mm layer of ballast over the bottom of the recess.

Sand
Always use sand that has been washed and is free from salt

Tamping
Tamp the square in both directions

3 Spread a thin layer of sand over the ballast and tamp it smooth with the beam. Repeat this several times, until the sand is well compacted and rises to within 70 mm of the level of the lawn.

Levelling
Level the bricks, both with each other and the surrounding lawn

Checking
Stand back to check that your layout of bricks is good

Gloves
Wear gloves to give you a better grip and to protect your hands

4 Position the bricks, bedding them lightly into the sand until they are level with the lawn and each other. Space the bricks to allow a generous joint between them for filling with sand.

Tamping
Apply even pressure across several bricks to bring them level without breaking them

5 When all the bricks have been laid, tamp them level with the beam and club hammer. Finally, brush sand in and around the bricks until the whole arrangement feels firm and stable.

Helpful hint

If you have difficulty brushing the dry sand into the joints between the bricks, use a hose to spray a fine mist of water over the whole arrangement so that the sand is washed into the gaps.

Woodland steps

These slow-rise steps are perfect for a gently sloping area. The green wood posts and poles, covered with bark, bring a touch of woodland atmosphere into your garden. You can imagine that, just hidden from view, there is a lush green forest glade waiting to be discovered. Chipped bark scattered on the treads contributes to the picture.

TIME

Two days' work (about a day and a half for building the basic structure, and the rest of the time for planting and tidying up).

SPECIAL TIP

If you have a small van or truck, the best way of getting the wood is to drive to the country and buy from a green wood outlet. These are generally relatively inexpensive.

YOU WILL NEED

Materials *for a flight of steps approximately 2 m long, and 3 m wide narrowing to 2 m (Apart from skinned and pointed poles, green wood is commonly sold to the nearest metre length.)*

- Green wood: 13 posts, 1 m long and 150 mm in diameter (to be cut in half for the 26 flanking piles)
- Green wood: 3 posts, 2 m long and 80 mm in diameter (treads)
- Green wood: 1 post, 3 m long and 80 mm in diameter (top tread)
- Green wood: 8 pointed poles, 300–500 mm long and 50 mm in diameter (tread supports)
- Plastic sheet: 6 m long and 1 m wide
- Gravel or ballast: 1 wheelbarrow load for each step
- Chipped bark: 1 wheelbarrow load for each step

Tools

- Crosscut saw
- Small axe
- Tape measure, pegs and string
- Spade
- Fork
- Wheelbarrow
- Sledgehammer
- Scissors

A WILD WALK

This project neatly solves the tricky problem of how to build steps without going to all the trouble of digging footings, mixing concrete and so on. To start, a narrow walkway is edged with green wood posts, and then the area within it is terraced. The building procedure is beautifully simple. The shape and width of the whole flight of steps is marked out on the ground, trenches are dug at the sides, and the flanking piles are positioned.

Tread posts are held in place by tread supports, which are banged into the ground until just lower than the tread. Each step consists of gravel and bark. If you want to make the flight of steps wider, or increase the number of steps, the project can be modified. It is possible to increase the depth of the steps from front to back, but the height of the risers needs to stay about the same.

PERSPECTIVE VIEW OF THE WOODLAND STEPS

Step-by-step: **Making the woodland steps**

Pile height
Go for a slightly staggered arrangement

Flanking trench
Dig the narrowest possible trench – no more than the width of the spade

Flanking pile
Try to get at least half the length of the pile set in the ground

1 Cut all the wood to length with the saw and axe. Use the tape measure, string and pegs to set out the two flanking trenches. Remove the turf and dig out the trenches to a depth of about 250 mm, keeping them as narrow as possible. Use the sledgehammer to knock the flanking piles into position.

Plastic sheet
Spike holes in the plastic to allow for drainage

2 Set the bottom tread in position and hammer in two tread supports with the sledgehammer. Position the second tread. Level the step with the sledgehammer. Cover with plastic sheet and lay down a layer of gravel and a layer of bark.

Helpful hint

If you are trying to cut costs, you can use scraps of plastic rather than new sheets. It does not matter what colour it is, as long as it is strong. Builders' merchants may be happy to let you have some old delivery bags.

Sledgehammer
Choose one that you can lift easily

Chipped bark
The bark can be mixed with wood chippings

Treads
Arrange the poles so there are no peaked areas of wood on the upper surface

3 Continue up the slope, positioning and fixing the treads, and spreading the plastic, gravel and chipped bark, all the while using the sledgehammer to tamp the steps level.

Sledgehammer
Always let the weight of the sledgehammer do the work

Alignment
Try to get the piles upright

Gravel
Compact the gravel into the trench around the base of the piles

4 Top up the flanking trenches with the remaining gravel (the trench to the lawn side of the posts) and tamp it level with the sledgehammer. Make sure the piles are upright and firmly in place.

Tread supports
The supports are slightly lower than the treads

Bark
As the bark settles, top it up if necessary

5 Use the weight of the sledgehammer to stamp the bark on each step level with its tread post. Aim for a smooth, compacted finish. The finished steps form a series of shallow terraces.

Rustic log ring path

Log rings sawn from a tree make an enchantingly rustic country path, which is perfect for a damp woodland setting. The meandering log rings, gravel and log roll edging harmonize beautifully with moist, lush borders. This path will complement any informal areas of garden, or blend naturally into a cottage-style garden.

TIME

Five hours (about an hour for each log ring).

SPECIAL TIPS

Ask your local woodland timber specialist for advice. It is best to buy a long-lasting wood such as oak or elm.

CROSS-SECTION OF THE RUSTIC LOG RING PATH

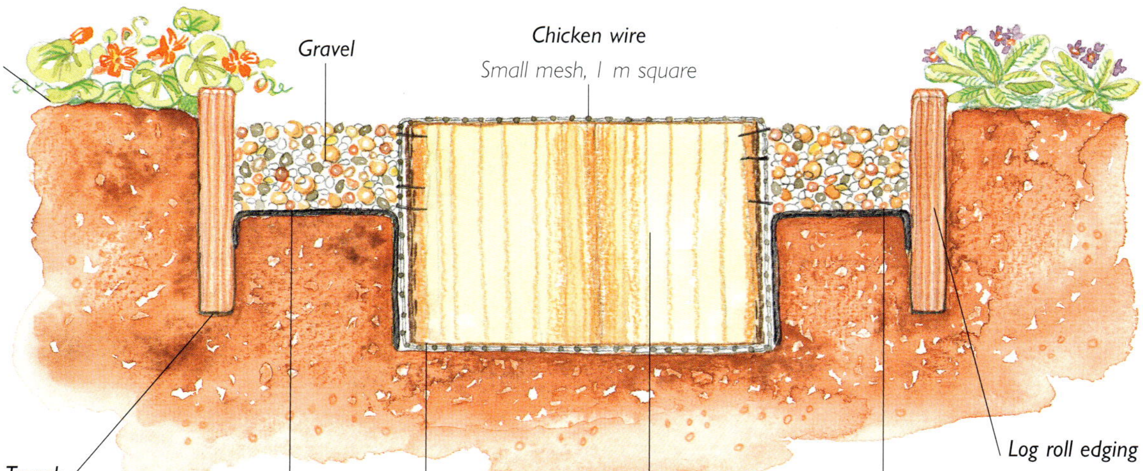

YOU WILL NEED

Materials *for a path about 4 m long*

- Log rings: 5 rings or slices about 500 mm in diameter and 300 mm thick (path)
- Log roll edging: 8 m long and about 300 mm high
- Plastic sheeting: 4 m long and 1 m wide
- Chicken wire: small-size mesh, about 1 sq. m for each log ring
- Gravel: about 2 wheelbarrow loads of washed gravel for each log slice
- Galvanized fencing staples: 1 kg of 20 mm-long staples

Tools

- Tape measure, pegs and a string line
- Spade
- Club hammer
- Wheelbarrow
- Craft knife
- Claw hammer
- Rake

LOG RING AROUND THE ROSES

If you are planning a rustic-style path, a log ring design is hard to beat. Not only does the path blend in with the borders and lawn right from the start, but as the log rings become covered with fungi and moss, the path begins to melt into the landscape.

When you have worked out the route of the path, see if you need to make any changes to the design and quantities. For example, do you want a much longer path? Or do you need to change the spacing of the log rings to suit the length of your stride? When it comes to choosing the log rings, it does not matter if they are different sizes and odd shapes, or even if they vary greatly in thickness from one to another, as long as each slice has one sound, level face. There are alternatives to using natural log rings, such as groups of smaller-diameter logs, cast concrete "logs", or short lengths of railway sleeper. Decorative or coloured gravel could be substituted for the natural type we have used.

The chicken wire used to cover the log rings provides a non-slip surface. It is folded and stapled to the log ring before it is put in place. When the path is completed and has settled, it's a good idea to fix the chicken wire with additional staples.

Step-by-step: **Making the rustic log ring path**

Log roll
Try to arrange in a smooth line

Depth
Use the club hammer to knock the log roll into place, so that 25 mm stands proud of ground level

1 Map out the course of the path with the tape measure, pegs and string. Dig a trench (the width of a spade and 275 mm deep) on each side of the path. Set the log roll edging in it, with the decorative side facing the path. The top should extend 25 mm above ground level.

Earth
Push earth into the trench on the flower border side and compact it to hold the log roll in place

Digging
Use the spade to chop around the shape of the log rings

2 Position the log rings along the course of the path, spacing them to suit your stride. Dig round each log ring and remove the turf. Clear the earth to create a log recess 325 mm deep. Excavate the rest of the path to make a gravel recess 125 mm deep. (See diagram on page 46 – measurements given represent the depth below ground level.)

Log spacing
Spend time making sure that the log rings are suitably positioned

3 Cover the whole width of the path with plastic sheet. Slash the sheet with the knife so that you can see the recesses for the log rings. Fold the slashed plastic down into the recesses. Make sure that there is plenty of room for the logs to fall through into the recesses.

4 Cover each log ring with chicken wire, tucking and folding it on the underside, and fix it in place with the claw hammer and staples. Fix the whole log parcel with enough staples to ensure that the wire on the upper face of the log is tight and smooth.

5 Set the log rings in position, bedding them down with the club hammer until they are stable and level. Finally, spread and rake a generous layer of gravel over the plastic, but leave the log rings standing proud.

Helpful hint

After a week or two, the ground will settle and both gravel and log rings may become uneven. If this happens, rake the gravel away from the log ring, lift it out, and put some gravel in the bottom of the hole. Replace the log and twist it level. Rake the gravel back around the edges.

Inspirations: Paths

Paths can be uniquely beautiful garden features. They are by their very nature a practical neccessity – perhaps a path from the front door to the gate or from the back door to the vegetable patch – but they can also inject pattern, colour and form into the garden. Many exciting effects can be created by using an imaginative combination of materials such as stone, brick, wood, cobbles, tiles, mosaic or decorative gravels, and giving careful thought to the surrounding planting.

RIGHT The beautifully designed paths in this country garden are an interesting contrast with the rugged countryside beyond.

ABOVE The low hedge encompassing this traditional brick path gives the feeling that this is a very private garden. On route to the bower seat, a lovely radiating pattern of random bricks encourages you to pause and admire the plants.

RIGHT (INSET) Stepping-stone paths and areas of gravel require little maintenance and complement an informal setting.

Natural patio

A quick yet eye-catching patio can be created by simply placing a geometric arrangement of flagstone slabs in the lawn, achieving a pleasing counterbalance between the stone and the grass. The spacing of the stones plumps up the grass between them to create a uniquely sumptuous, cushion-like effect.

TIME

Four hours (for nine flagstones).

SPECIAL TIP

Setting out the position of the flagstones is all-important, so don't rush the measuring-out stage.

YOU WILL NEED

Materials *for a patio 2.44 m square*
- Flagstones: 9 concrete or natural flags, 460 mm square and 50 mm thick, slate grey
- Edging stones: 44 reconstituted stone blocks, 450 mm long, 150 mm wide and 65 mm thick, buff colour with a natural edge (sunken edging)
- Builder's or soft sand: about 1 bucketful of sand per flagstone

Tools
- Wheelbarrow
- Tape measure
- Ball of twine and 16 pegs
- Spade
- Gardening trowel
- Bolster chisel
- Club hammer
- Fork

FAIR AND SQUARE

If you are looking for a patio project that involves the minimum of expertise, cost and work, yet you want to create a really stunning garden feature, this is the one to go for. It is designed to be set directly into an existing lawn, so you can have an instant, hard-wearing patio area without the need for hardcore and concrete. When the lawn needs mowing, you can run the lawnmower straight over the slabs without a problem.

The success of the design hinges on the relationship between the size of the slabs and the width of the grass between them, which achieves a plump, springy appearance. If the slabs were any wider apart, they would be mere stepping stones, while if they were any closer, the strips of grass would be insignificant.

Instead of using the patio as a seating area, you could use it as a unique design feature by placing a continually changing selection of plants in attractive pots on the slabs.

PERSPECTIVE VIEW OF THE NATURAL PATIO

Step-by-step: **Making the natural patio**

Measuring
The success of the project hinges on careful measuring

Squaring
It is vital that the slabs are square to each other

1 Lay out the flagstones and edging stones in the proposed position on the lawn. See how the arrangement looks in relation to the overall garden design.

Edging stones
Put some edging stones side by side to check the width of the trench that will be required

Checking
Double-check all the measurements before you make cuts in the grass

Right angles
Make sure that the slabs are square with the edging

2 Having made sure that the slabs are 200 mm apart and square with each other, use the pegs and twine to set out the trench for the edging. The lines of string should be 130 mm apart and set 200 mm away from the slabs.

Digging
Hold the spade upright to cut accurate trenches

Pegs
The pegs are positioned back from the corners

Waste earth
Remove the excavated earth from the site so that it does not spoil the grass

3 Dig out the trench with the spade and trowel, making it 150 mm deep and 130 mm wide. Do your best to keep the trench crisp and clean-sided, and avoid damaging the grass. Remove debris from the site in the wheelbarrow.

Level
Set the stones ever so slightly lower than the lawn

Corners
Stagger the stones so that the joints are offset

4 Set the edging stones end to end in the trench, so that the top face is flush with the level of the lawn. (To cut the stones, set the bolster chisel on the mark and give it a smart blow with the club hammer.)

Helpful hint

Do your best to keep the site clear of earth and debris. To this end try to work on dry days, and avoid trickling earth over the grass. You might also consider standing on work boards to protect the grass, and wiping your shoes to remove mud.

Crisp cut
Aim for clean-sided holes

5 To fit the flagstones, slice around the slab with the spade, remove the turf with the fork and dig out a recess to a depth of about 60 mm. Spread sand over the base of the recess and carefully bed the slab in position, so that it is level with the lawn. Repeat this procedure for all the slabs.

Sand
Spread a layer of sand in the hole. Make it thick enough to bring the slab up to the level of the lawn

Green wood walkway

A green wood walkway is not only a practical solution to how best to run a path over boggy, wet ground, but it is also an exciting and dynamic structure, rather like a bridge or a seaside pier. And, just like a seaside pier, you will find that the walkway soon becomes a focus and an attraction in its own right.

TIME

An easy weekend (about four hours to plan and prepare the site and the rest of the time for the woodwork).

SPECIAL TIP

Do your best to get uniform-section wood (all the same diameter), as it will make the project much easier.

YOU WILL NEED

Materials *for a walkway 2.686 m long and 900 mm wide. (Apart from skinned and pointed poles, green wood is commonly sold to the nearest metre length.)*

- Green wood: 30 skinned posts, 2 m long and 70 mm in diameter (all the component parts)
- Galvanized chicken wire: 3 m long and 1 m wide (to make an anti-slip surface on the walkway)
- Steel nails: 3 kg pack of 150 mm x 6 mm
- Galvanized fencing staples: 0.5 kg of 20 mm-long staples (for fixing the chicken wire)

Tools

- Tape measure, pegs and string
- Sledgehammer
- Spirit level
- Portable workbench
- Crosscut saw
- Axe
- Wooden mallet
- Cordless electric drill with a drill bit to match the nail size
- Claw hammer

CROSS-SECTION OF THE GREEN WOOD WALKWAY

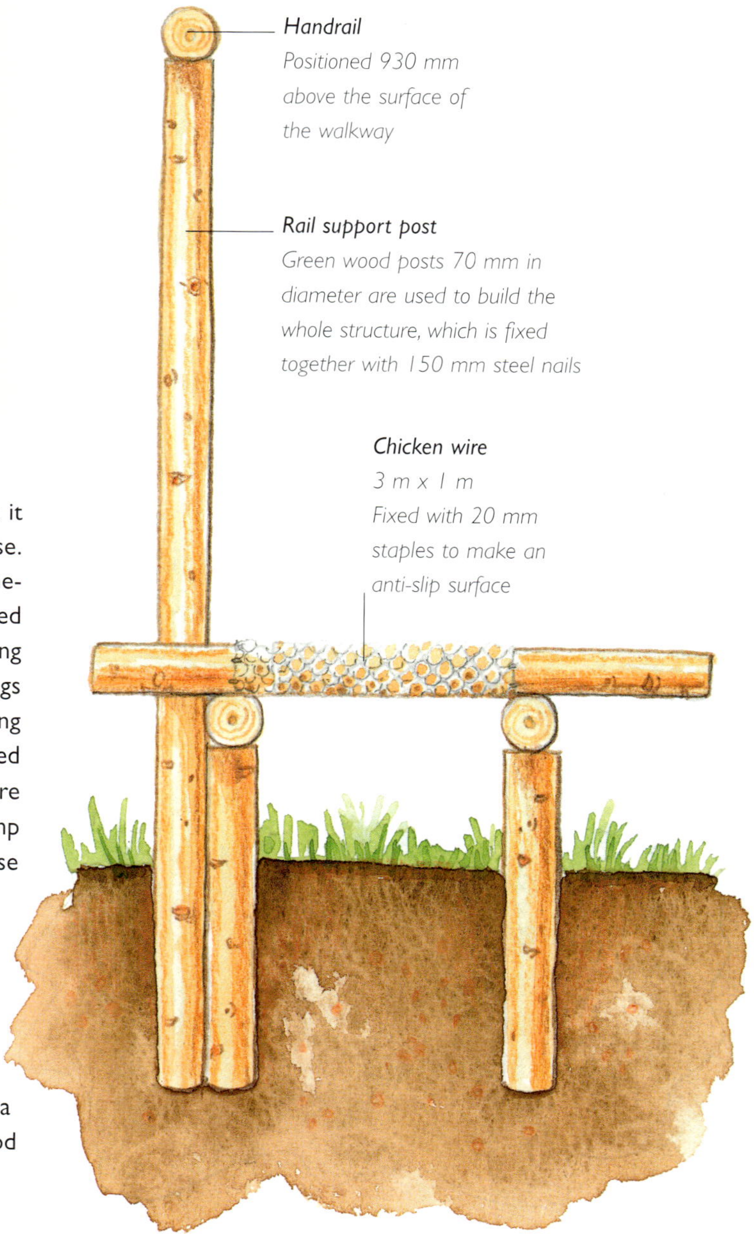

AN ABSOLUTE WALKOVER

You might think that a raised walkway is not very exciting, but it is in fact a most exhilarating structure both to build and to use. We found that the moment the walkway was completed, it immediately invited attention. Children started playing on it, aged relations liked the fact that it was level with a good handrail, young friends seemed to want to test out its strength, and even our dogs and cats appreciated it as a place to enjoy the sun. The building process is straightforward because there are no complicated joints to cut – instead, identical green wood round sections are sawn and nailed to each other. For bridging a patch of damp ground or perhaps a bumpy area, this is a good project to choose if you would like a structure that is a little out of the ordinary.

If the ground levels at each end of the proposed walkway are wildly different, it may be necessary to have a step at one end. If you want the walkway to go round a corner, simply build a second walkway that leads at right angles from the first, rather than attempting to incorporate a gradual bend.

To ensure that the completed walkway has a long life, it's a good idea to give the whole structure a coat of general wood preservative in the colour of your choice.

Green wood walkway

PERSPECTIVE VIEW OF THE GREEN WOOD WALKWAY

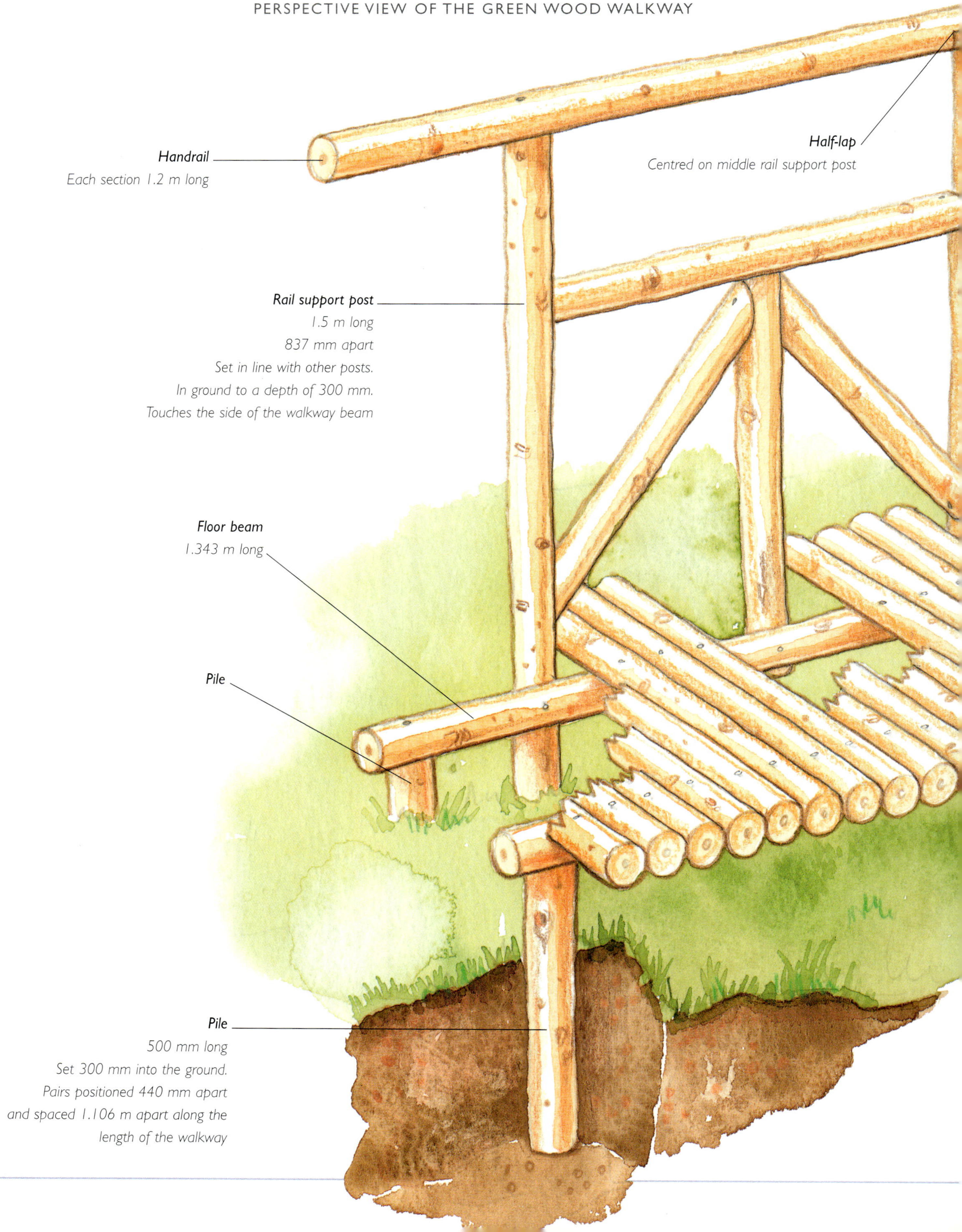

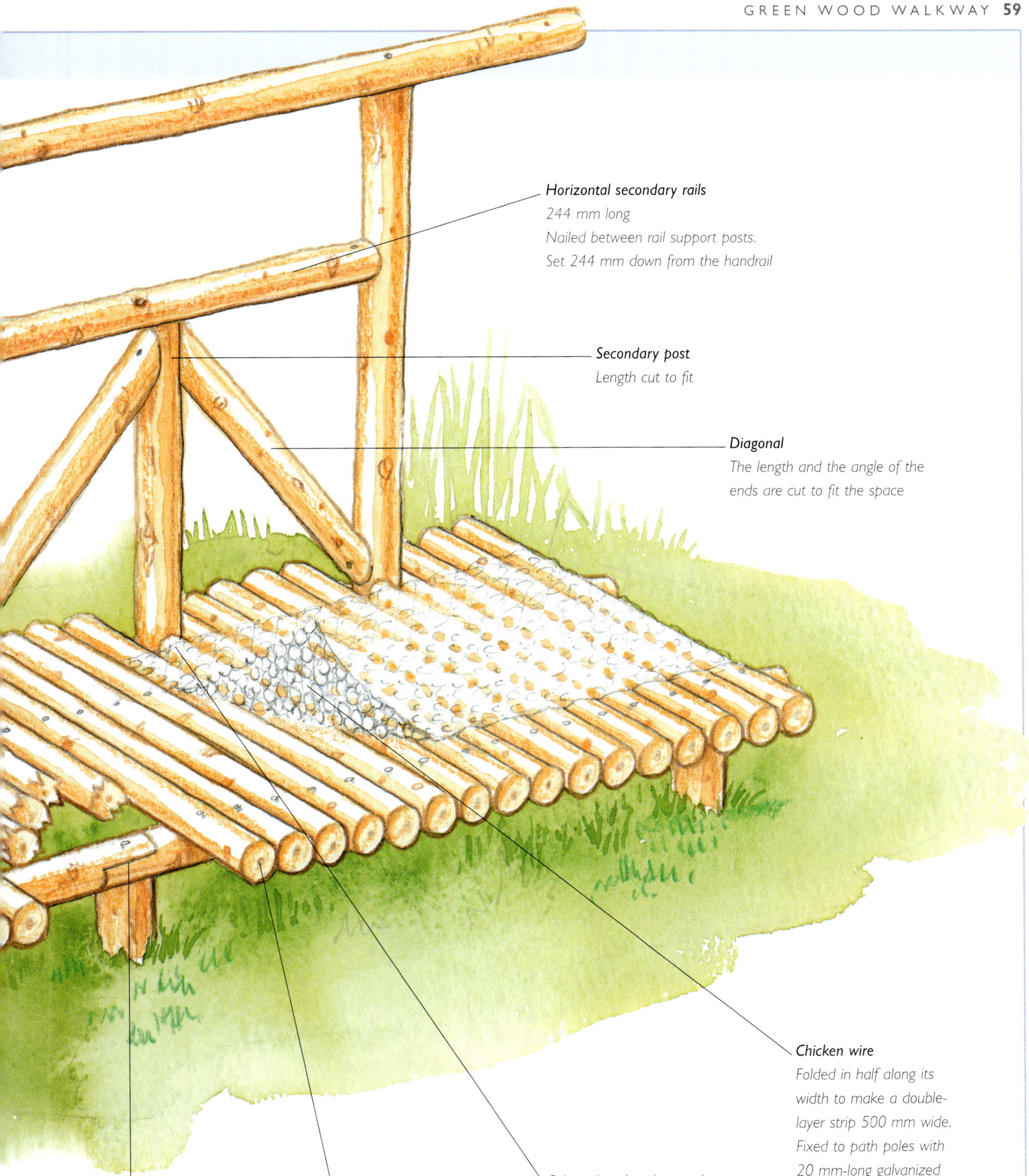
Horizontal secondary rails
244 mm long
Nailed between rail support posts.
Set 244 mm down from the handrail
Secondary post
Length cut to fit
Diagonal
The length and the angle of the ends are cut to fit the space
Chicken wire
Folded in half along its width to make a double-layer strip 500 mm wide. Fixed to path poles with 20 mm-long galvanized fencing staples
Selected path poles need to be notched or cut back in length to fit around the upright posts
Path pole
900 mm long
Half-lap
Joins the walkway beams. Centred on the middle pair of piles

Step-by-step: **Making the green wood walkway**

1 Mark out the site with the tape measure, pegs and string. Cut six 500 mm-long piles and knock them into the ground with the sledgehammer to a depth of 300 mm. Each pair of piles is 440 mm apart. The distance between each pair along the length of the walkway is 1.106 m. Check with the spirit level and make adjustments until the piles are level.

2 Take four 1.343 m lengths to make the floor beams. Use the saw, axe and mallet to cut a half-lap on one end of each beam. Lap the beams so that they are centred on the middle pair of piles. Drill pilot holes and nail the beams in place with the claw hammer. Work carefully to avoid splitting the wood.

3 Cut three 1.5 m-long rail support posts. Set them in line and 837 mm apart (so that all three posts are centred on and touching the side of the floor beam), and bang them into the ground with the sledgehammer to a depth of 300 mm.

4 Prepare the handrail from two 1.2 m lengths of wood. Cut a half-lap on one end of each, then nail in place so that the lapped joint is centred on the middle rail support post. Drive the nails just below the surface of the wood to ensure that the handrail is smooth to the touch.

5 Take two 244 mm lengths and nail them between the three rail support posts to make the horizontal secondary rails. Set the rails about 244 mm down from the handrail. Cut and nail the secondary posts in place. Use the spirit level to ensure that the horizontal secondary rails and handrail are level.

6 Cut diagonals to fit, and nail them between the upright posts and below the secondary rails to make the inverted "V" pattern. Hammer the nails in at an angle, so that they are more or less at right angles to the face of the diagonals. You might need help to hold the diagonals while you drive in the nails.

7 Cut 33 path poles, 900 mm long, and nail them on top of the floor beams. Note how selected poles need to be cut back to fit around the upright posts. Arrange the poles so that their best face is uppermost, and they fit together well.

8 Fold the chicken wire in half along its width, so that it is doubled up to make a strip 500 mm wide. Fix it to the surface of the walkway with staples. The double layer of wire provides a much better non-slip surface than a single layer.

Classic stone sett patio

The pleasing thing about using stone setts is that they can be positioned with the minimum of fuss – it really is as near instant as it is possible to be. Dry-mix mortar is brushed between the imitation stone setts to complete the illusion. If you want to replicate a little bit of Victorian Britain, this is the project to go for.

TIME

A long weekend (about eight hours to prepare the site and lay the concrete, and the rest of the time for positioning the slabs, fitting the edging and tidying up).

SAFETY

The stone setts are sharp-edged on the underside, so wear gloves and handle them with care.

YOU WILL NEED

Materials

for a patio 2.1 m x 1.3 m

- Reconstituted stone 'circle' paving setts: 100 component parts 80–90 mm wide and 50 mm thick, charcoal colour (enough to make a complete circle motif at about 1 m in diameter)
- Reconstituted stone 'straight' paving setts: 200 component parts, 80–90 mm square and 50 mm thick, charcoal colour (enough to add around the circle, to make a total layout that measures 2 m long and 1.2 m wide)
- Rope-top edging: 12 edging components, 600 mm long, 150 mm high and 50 mm thick, terracotta colour (to frame and contain the paving)
- Pillar and ball posts: 4 posts, 280 mm high and 60 mm square, terracotta colour (to link the rope edging at the corners)
- Hardcore: about 8 wheelbarrow loads of builder's rubble or crushed stone waste
- Concrete: 1 part (35 kg) cement, 2 parts (70 kg) sharp sand, 3 parts (105 kg) aggregate
- Mortar: 1 part (100 kg) cement, 3 parts (300 kg) builder's or soft sand
- Dry-mix mortar: 1 part (24 kg) cement, 3 parts (72 kg) builder's or soft sand

Tools

- Tape measure, straight-edge and a piece of chalk
- Spade and shovel
- Spirit level
- String line and pegs
- Formwork: wooden battens about 50 mm wide and 30 mm thick, long enough to edge all sides of the patio
- Sledgehammer
- Wheelbarrow and bucket
- Tamping beam: about 1.5 m long, 60 mm wide and 30 mm thick
- Bricklayer's trowel
- Angle grinder fitted with a stone-cutting disc
- Bolster chisel
- Club hammer
- Broom and brush

A MAGIC SETT PIECE

The wonderful thing about stone setts is the ease with which they can be put down. With the minimum of effort and expertise the setts can be swiftly arranged into a really convincing Victorian paving feature. The individual setts are simply bedded in sand and grouted so that they form a unified whole.

Ideally, the setts need to be set flat on a concrete slab and framed with rope-top edging. We have chosen to make a small patio on an existing area of chipped bark, but you could just as well use the product to disguise an existing concrete patio, or even to create a little sitting area in the middle of a lawn. We have used the setts to make a circle motif set within a rectangle; but alternatively, you could have several linked circles, or omit the circle and go for strips. We recommend that you visit a builder's yard to see the product, study our designs, and then carefully select the various setts so that they can be positioned with the minimum of cutting. You will see that the setts are basically square, rectilinear and triangular.

CROSS-SECTION OF THE CLASSIC CARPET STONE PATIO

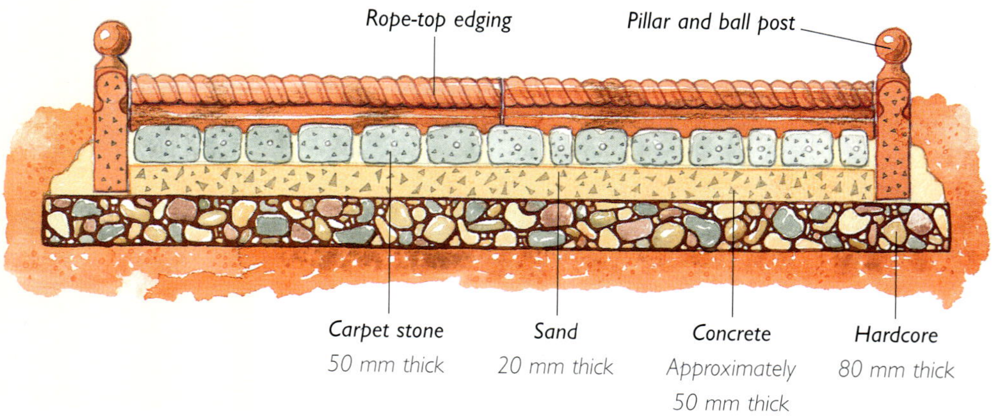

Classic stone sett patio

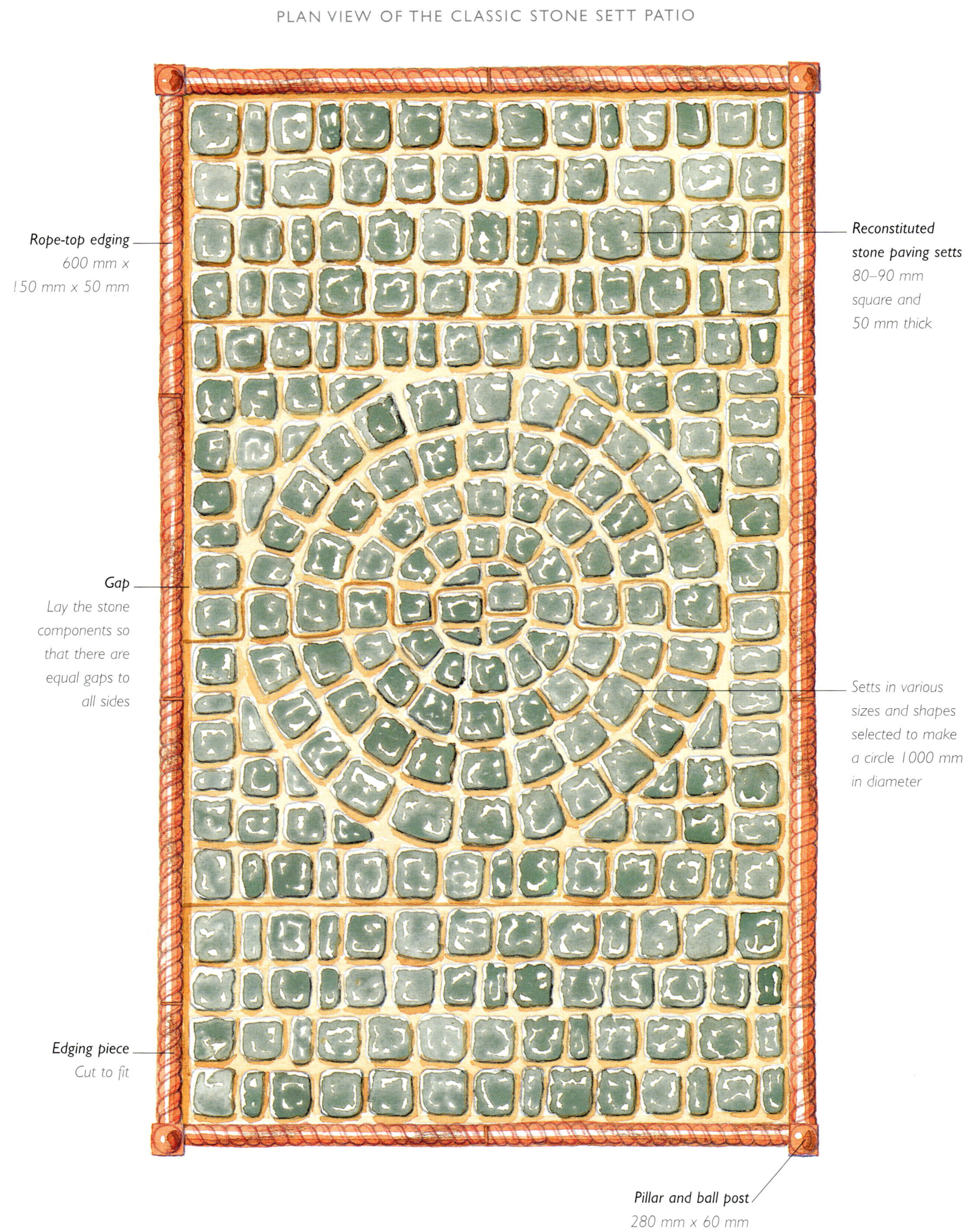

EXPLODED VIEW OF THE CLASSIC STONE SETT PATIO

Step-by-step: **Making the classic stone sett patio**

1 Use a spade and spirit level to level an area measuring 2.5 m x 1.5 m. Spread an 80 mm-thick layer of hardcore over it and peg out the formwork to make a frame 2.03 m long and 1.23 m wide. Compact the hardcore with the sledgehammer. Pay particular attention to the corner areas and edges.

2 Mix the concrete and pour it into the frame. Use the beam to tamp the concrete level with the top of the wood. Leave to set overnight. If rain threatens, cover it with plastic sheet; if there is likely to be a frost, cover it with sacking or layers of newspaper.

3 When the concrete has set, remove the formwork. Spread a 20 mm layer of sand over the concrete and carefully arrange the setts into position.

Helpful hint

When you are putting the stone setts in position, spend time carefully arranging them for best overall fit. If you have to cut the setts, then use the angle grinder, bolster chisel and club hammer – in much the same way as when cutting the rope-top edging.

Edging
Use a spirit level to make checks on the edging

Corners
Ensure that the corner posts are upright

4 Starting at one corner of the patio, position the pillar and ball posts and the rope-top edging. Set them in a stiff mix of mortar (the bottom of the rope detail running along the top of the edging should be slightly higher than the surface of the stone setts). Clean off any stray mortar that has dropped on the edging and setts.

Hammer blows
Make little taps rather than big ones

Wood block
Place under the stone to give an even surface to work on

Angle grinder
Make the scored line over the rope detail extra-deep

5 To cut a piece of rope-top edging, place it on a wooden board, draw a chalk line to establish the line of cut and score it with the angle grinder. Set the bolster chisel in the groove and tap with the club hammer until the edging breaks.

Surface
You must wait until the surface is dry before filling the gaps

Brush
Use a soft-bristled brush to tease the mortar into the joints

6 Finally, make a pile of dry-mix mortar and use the broom and brush to spread it over the stone setts, filling all the joints. Continue until all the joints are full. This procedure must be carried out on a dry day.

Art Deco steps

The exciting thing about the Art Deco steps is that they lead your eye from one level of the garden to another, and beckon you to take the route that they offer. These attractive steps are just asking to be embellished with plants to add to their charm.

TIME

A whole weekend (one day for levelling the ground, digging the trench and laying the foundation, and the rest of the time for the stonework and the slabs).

SPECIAL TIP

This is a backbreaking project, so it might be a good idea to get some help, or perhaps spread the work over two weekends.

YOU WILL NEED

Materials *for 8 steps spanning 2.8 m and rising 600 mm*

- Outer segment paving stones: 8 radius slabs, 455 mm long, 355 mm wide at the narrow end, 535 mm wide at the broad end, and about 50 mm thick (purchase slabs designed to be used as the outer ring of a circular paving kit for a patio about 2.5 m in diameter)
- Split stone (sandstone or limestone): about 5 wheelbarrow loads
- Broken brick and/or stone waste: about 2 wheelbarrow loads
- Hardcore for the foundation (either stone waste or builder's rubble): 4 wheelbarrow loads
- Cobbles and stones for decoration: quantity to suit
- Concrete: 1 part (25 kg) cement, 2 parts (50 kg) sharp sand, 3 parts (75 kg) aggregate
- Mortar: 2 parts (50 kg) cement, 1 part (25 kg) lime, 9 parts (225 kg) soft sand

Tools

- Tape measure, pegs and string line
- Wooden levelling pegs: 10 pegs, 200 mm long
- Spade, shovel, wheelbarrow
- Sledgehammer
- Spirit level
- Tamping beam: about 355 mm long, 60 mm wide and 20 mm thick
- Mason's hammer
- Club hammer
- Bricklayer's trowel
- Pointing trowel

ONE STEP AT A TIME

Walk around your garden and see if there is an area that might benefit from a curved flight of about half a dozen steps – perhaps from the lawn to the patio, or from the house down to the garden. If your garden is pretty much all at the same level, like ours, you might even want to move in a tonne or so of earth to create a mound especially for some steps.

Bear in mind that if each step slab is 50 mm thick and positioned up from the neighbouring step by 25 mm, and if one step laps over another by about 100 mm, then a flight of eight steps adds up to a total vertical rise of about 600 mm, and a horizontal distance of 2.8 m. Study your garden in terms of the flow of human traffic, to decide where the steps might best be placed. When you have made sure that the area is free from drain covers and suchlike, you can get down to work.

SIDE VIEW OF THE ART DECO STEPS

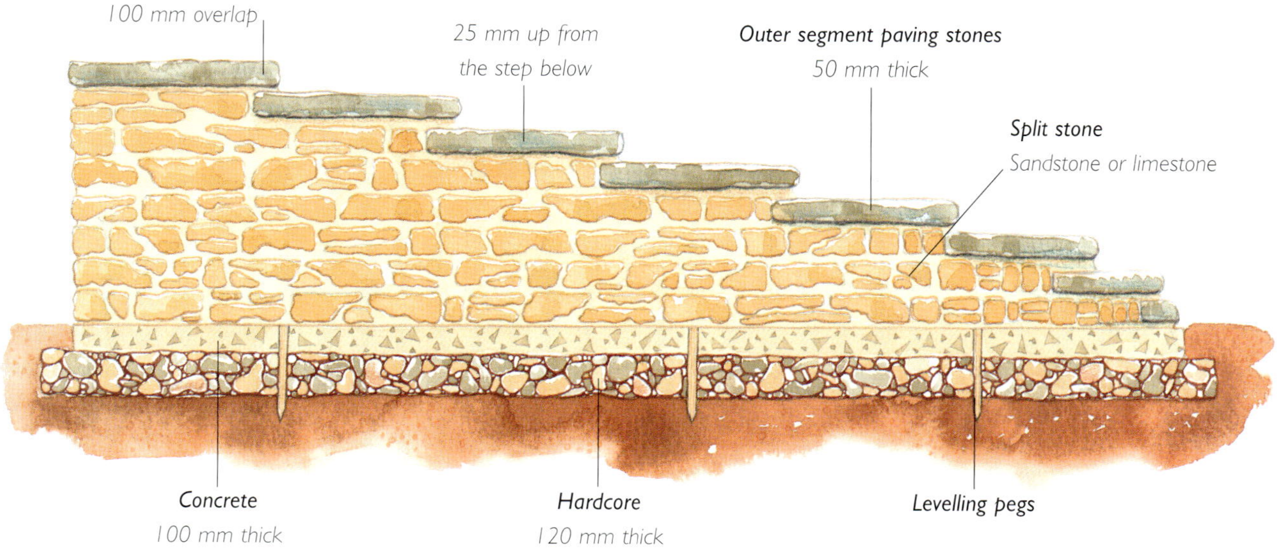

Art Deco steps

PERSPECTIVE VIEW OF THE ART DECO STEPS

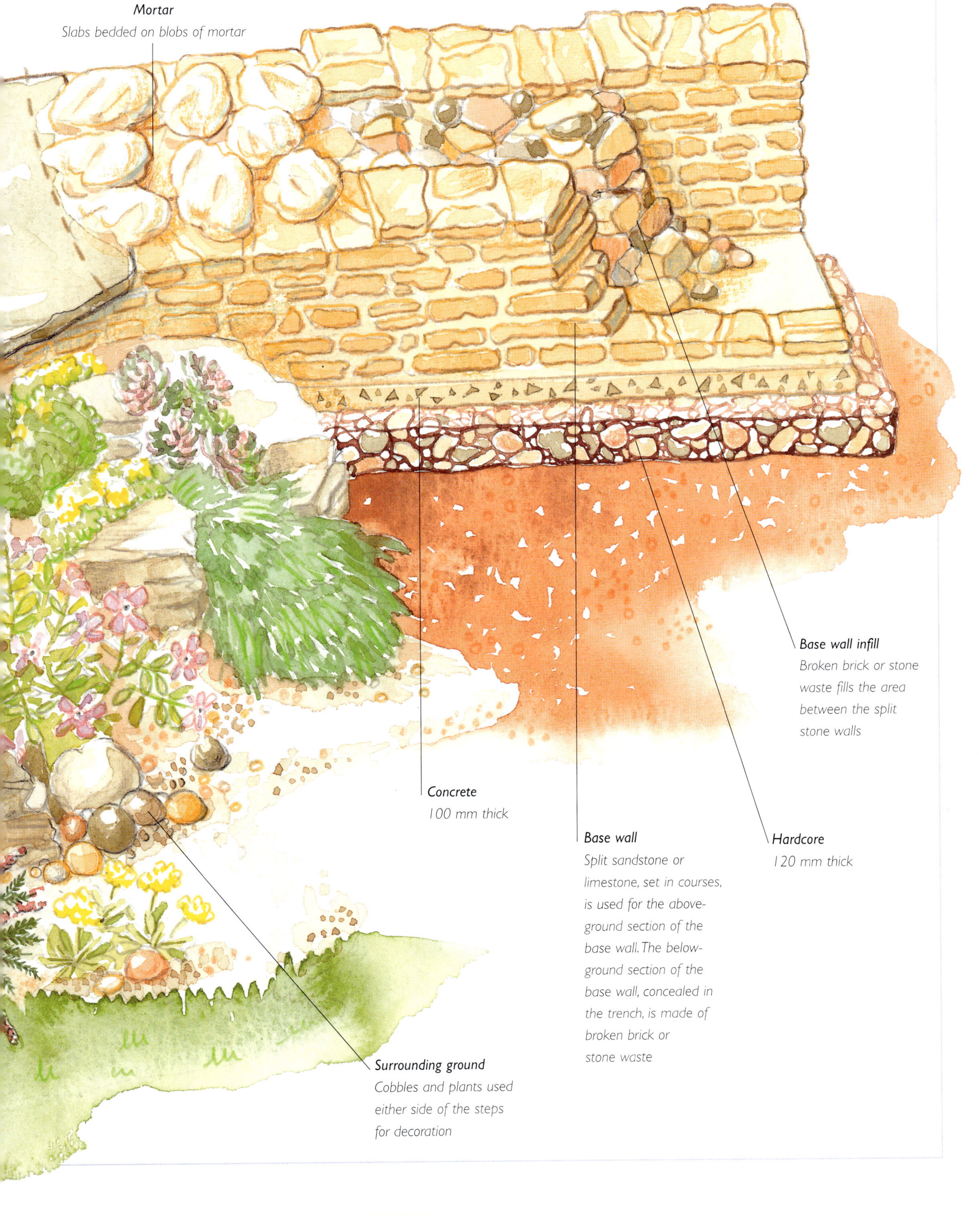

Mortar
Slabs bedded on blobs of mortar
Base wall infill
Broken brick or stone waste fills the area between the split stone walls
Concrete
100 mm thick
Base wall
Split sandstone or limestone, set in courses, is used for the above-ground section of the base wall. The below-ground section of the base wall, concealed in the trench, is made of broken brick or stone waste
Hardcore
120 mm thick
Surrounding ground
Cobbles and plants used either side of the steps for decoration

Step-by-step: **Making the Art Deco steps**

1 Mark out the position of the steps with pegs and string. Clear the earth so it is level with the bottom step, and dig out a trench to match the area of the whole flight of steps, making it 355 mm wide and 300 mm deep. Spread a 120 mm layer of hardcore, and compact and level it with the sledgehammer. Check that it is level with the spirit level. Hammer in levelling pegs along the trench, extending 100 mm above the hardcore, about 900 mm apart. Check that they are level with the spirit level. Pour in a 100 mm layer of concrete, tamping it level with the beam. Leave to set overnight.

2 Using the bricklayer's trowel, bed the radius slab for the bottom step on dabs of mortar. For the next step, lay a layer of broken brick and/or stone waste in the trench (to match the size of the slab), making a base wall that finishes up about 20 mm higher than the first step slab. Throughout, the mason's and club hammers are used for breaking stone and tapping it into position. Spread a generous layer of mortar over the base wall, and then very carefully position and bed the second step slab so that it laps over the first.

Infill
The middle of the wall is made from stone waste or broken brick

Base wall
To ensure that the above-ground part of the wall looks its best, build with care for decorative effect

Best face
Use the best stone for the face of the wall that is on view

3 As soon as the base wall rises above the level of the trench, it is on show and so is constructed with outer walls of split stone, mortared together, and a central infill of broken brick and stone waste.

Pointing
Undercut the pointing under the front edge of the steps

4 With mortar and pointing trowel, use the split stone to build up the base wall so that it is 20 mm higher than the second step, and then bed the third step in place as already described. Repeat the process for the remainder of the steps.

Helpful hint

When you are putting the slabs in position, be careful that you don't knock the walls askew – you may need help. If the weather is hot and dry, dampen the underside of the slabs prior to bedding them on the mortar.

Inspirations: Steps

The beauty of a flight of steps is that you can use it to make a design statement above and beyond its practical purpose as a means of climbing from one level to another. The wealth of materials available means that you can create something of rustic simplicity or elegant formality, or have fun with pattern and colour. Steps can create a swirl of movement that links different areas into an interconnected whole.

ABOVE A flight of railway sleeper steps lined by banks of lavender. The flowers will release their fragrance as people brush past. A simple, effective design.

RIGHT A semicircular flight of steps to a doorway, with brick risers and crazy-paved treads. Note how the top riser is built using half-bricks.

ABOVE Wide, moss-covered steps grandly lead the way up to an old country house. Their time-worn, velvety appearance establishes this as a place with a history. Although they look beautiful, the steps have one drawback – in damp weather they are liable to become very slippery and hazardous.

Elizabethan half-circle doorstep

A doorstep is a functional way of moving from one level to another (in this case from the garden into the house) but it can also be an attractive feature in its own right. The ornate decoration of this particular step is reminiscent of knot gardens and pretty posies – perfect for those who are romantics at heart.

TIME

A weekend (one day for the basic brickwork, and the rest of the time for setting the slab and for pointing).

SPECIAL TIP

Put all the bits of bricks and dry mortar in the step before you top it up with concrete.

CROSS-SECTION OF THE ELIZABETHAN HALF-CIRCLE DOORSTEP

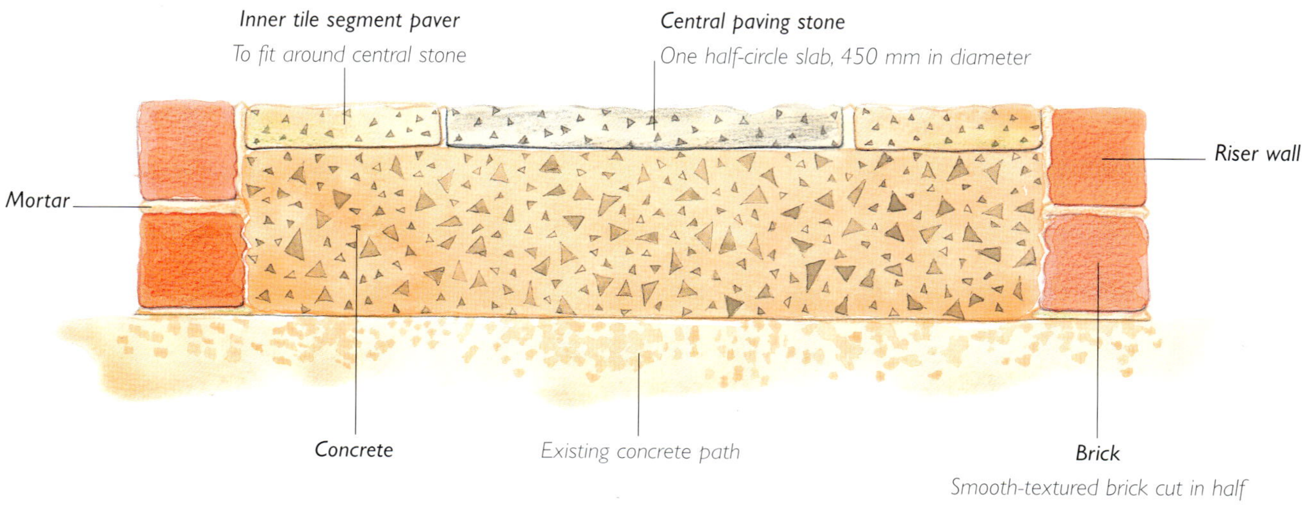

YOU WILL NEED

Materials *for a doorstep 1.17 m in diameter and 225 mm high*

- Central paving stone:
  1 half-circle slab, 450 mm in diameter, 40 mm thick
- Inner tile segments:
  2 segments, internal diameter to fit around central paving stone (with 10–20 mm gap allowed), external diameter 910 mm, 40 mm thick
- Bricks: 25 smooth-textured red bricks
- Mortar:
  2 parts (10 kg) cement,
  1 part (5 kg) lime,
  9 parts (45 kg) soft sand
- Concrete:
  1 part (15 kg) cement,
  2 parts (30 kg) sharp sand,
  3 parts (45 kg) aggregate

Tools

- Tape measure and a piece of chalk
- Bolster chisel
- Club hammer
- Wheelbarrow
- Bucket
- Bricklayer's trowel
- Spirit level
- Pointing trowel
- Shovel
- Soft-bristled hand brush

MAKING A GRAND ENTRANCE

This project draws its inspiration from Victorian steps, which themselves were influenced by steps that were made in England during the Elizabethan period. The steps are characterized by the use of a mixture of red brick and low-fired brick tiles set on edge. We have modified the design by using two inner "tile-on-edge pavers", plus a central stone paver (items really intended to be used as part of a radius paving patio kit).

The step is constructed in four stages – cutting and laying the bricks, back-filling with concrete behind the riser wall, setting the pavers in place, and pointing the joints. We were able to build the step straight off an existing concrete path, but you might have to start by laying a concrete base slab.

Cutting the bricks in half is much easier than it looks – one good blow with the club hammer and the bolster chisel usually does the job. Just be confident and brave! However, if you would prefer not to cut bricks, or simply want to slash costs, use either salvaged half-bricks or bricks that have been broken in transit. Most suppliers are able to provide broken bricks. Failing that, you could build the riser wall from whole bricks standing on end.

Elizabethan half-circle doorstep

PERSPECTIVE VIEW OF THE ELIZABETHAN HALF-CIRCLE DOORSTEP

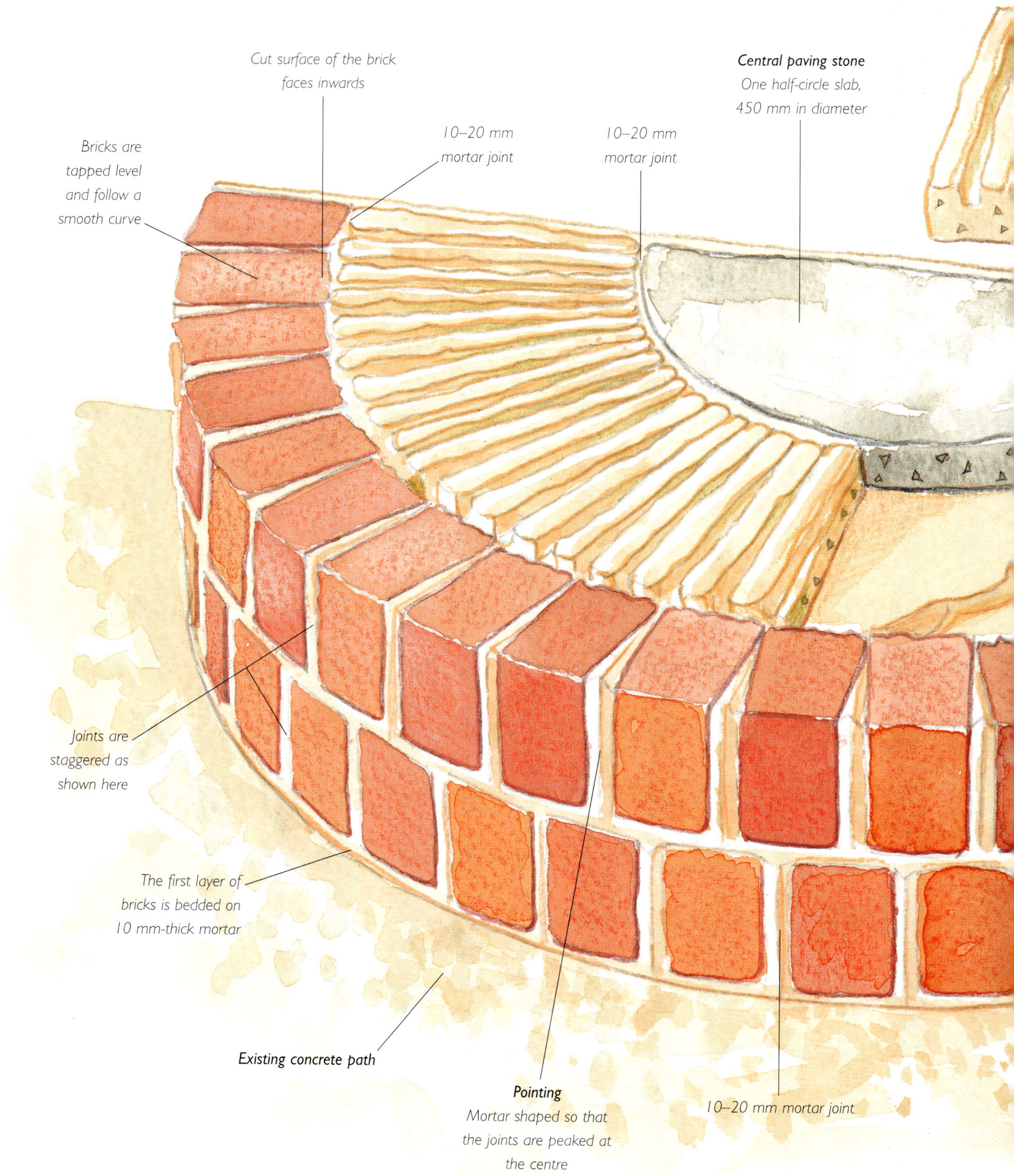

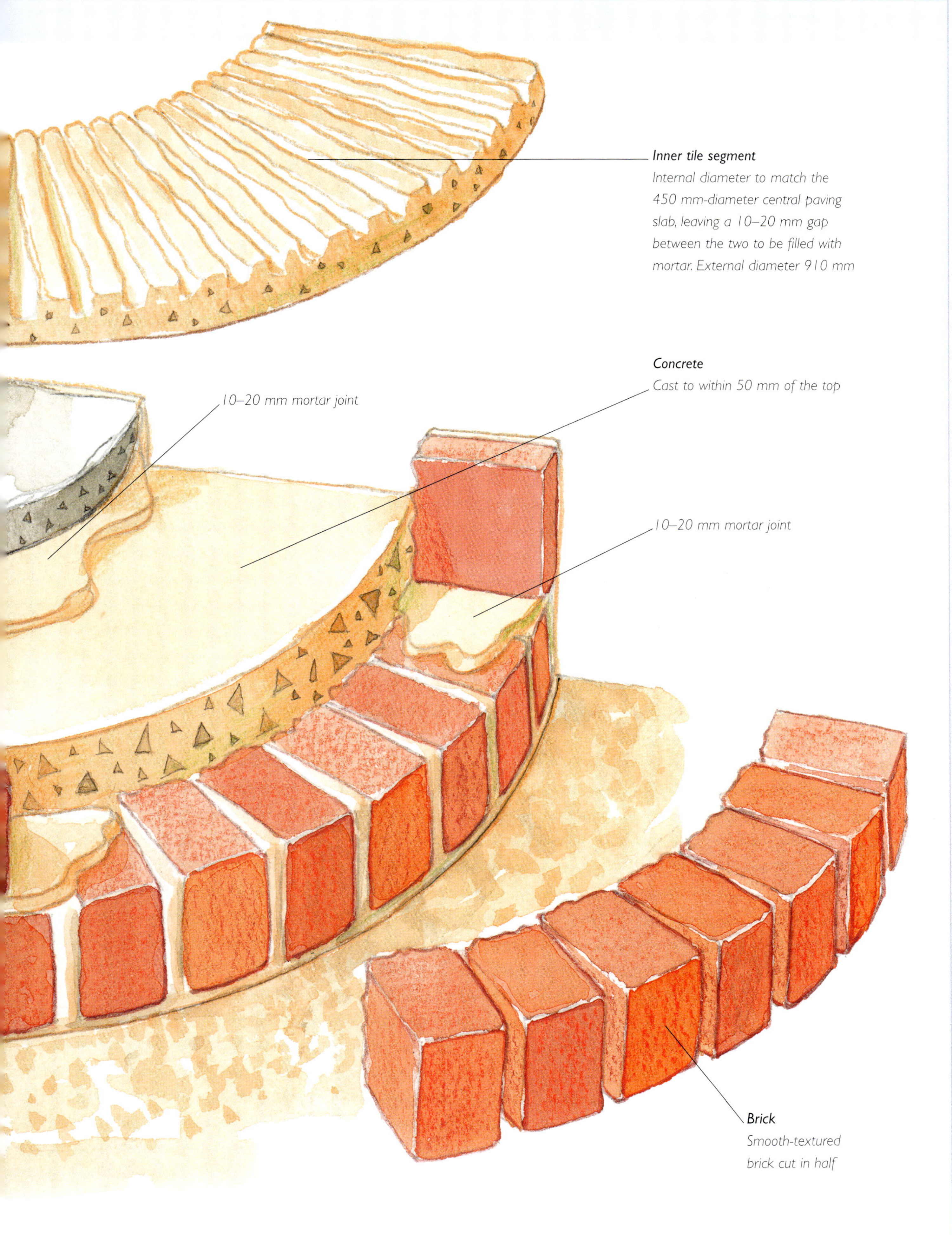

Inner tile segment
Internal diameter to match the 450 mm-diameter central paving slab, leaving a 10–20 mm gap between the two to be filled with mortar. External diameter 910 mm
Concrete
Cast to within 50 mm of the top
10–20 mm mortar joint
10–20 mm mortar joint
Brick
Smooth-textured brick cut in half

Step-by-step: **Making the Elizabethan half-circle doorstep**

Central paving stone
Align the half-circle with the centre of the doorway

Brick
Use the brick's width to draw out the border

1 Carefully centre the half-circle central paving stone and the two inner tile segments outside the door. Use a brick and chalk to draw the border around the tiles to the correct width.

Helpful hint

If possible, use hand-made red clay bricks rather than machine-made bricks, which tend to be very dense and so do not break as easily. This project requires a lot of half-bricks, so it is important that you can break them with ease. Avoid extruded bricks with holes through them and concrete bricks.

Layout
Arrange the bricks so that the gaps are wedge-shaped in top view

Best face
Position the half-bricks so that the best end is on view

2 Use the bolster chisel and the club hammer to break the bricks in half, until you have about 40 half-bricks. Set out the bricks (dry) so that they are standing on edge with the best end faces looking to the front and the broken ends hidden from view on the inside.

Waste mortar
Scrape all the waste mortar into the half-circle

Tapping
Tap the bricks into position using the handle of the trowel

Dampening
Moisten the bricks prior to laying in place

3 Remove the pavers and wet the half-bricks. Mix a stiff mortar with the bricklayer's trowel and lay the bricks to form the riser wall – one line upon another with the vertical joints staggered, and with the ends set true to the centre of the circle. Check with the spirit level.

Surface joint
The joint must be wedge-shaped in top view

Pointing trowel
Use the edge of the trowel to smooth the face of the mortar

Face joint
The peak must divide the width of the joint equally

4 Use the pointing trowel to first rake out the joints to a depth of about 20 mm, and then to top them up with fresh mortar. Point the mortar so that the vertical joints are "peaked" at the centre.

Tamping
Use the weight of the hammer to level the tiles

Mortar
Butter fresh mortar over the concrete

5 Fill the recess behind the riser wall with concrete, to within 50 mm of the top. When the concrete has begun to set, butter it with fresh mortar and bed the half-circle and the inner tile segments in place. Check with the spirit level.

Pointing trowel
Use the point of the trowel to sculpt the mortar

Pointing
The mortar emphasises the shape of the inner tile segments

Mortar
Wait 48 hours for the mortar to cure before using the step

6 Mix a small amount of fresh mortar and use the pointing trowel to tidy up all the joints seen on the top face. Finally, use the soft brush to remove mortar from the faces of the pavers and bricks, working with a flicking action.

Decorative Victorian path

This project is particularly suitable for a traditional Victorian townhouse with a small front garden. If you enjoy colour and geometric patterns, and are planning a straight path from the gate to the front door, this classic formal path will create a striking feature. The durable materials are good for a front path, which will get a lot of use.

TIME

Three days (two days for making the foundation and one day for setting the slabs, edging, and tidying up).

SAFETY

Cement can cause skin irritation and burns – always wear gloves for mixing. Use a barrier cream as well if your skin is sensitive.

YOU WILL NEED

Materials *for a path 5 m long and 950 mm wide.*

- Paving slabs or tiles – either reconstituted stone or clay terracotta: 36 tiles, 300 x 300 mm square and 38 mm thick (18 slate grey and 18 brick red)
- Border setts: concrete Victorian paving stone setts: 22 sections, 460 mm long, 160 mm wide and 38 mm thick (side of the path)
- Edging tiles: 30 concrete or glazed ceramic Victorian tiles, 230 mm high, 190 mm wide and 30 mm thick (to edge one side of the path)
- Hardcore (builder's rubble or waste stone): about 10 wheelbarrow loads
- Pea gravel: about 2 wheelbarrow loads
- Mortar: 1 part (24 kg) cement, 2 parts (48 kg) soft sand
- Concrete: 1 part (70 kg) cement, 2 parts (140 kg) sharp sand, 3 parts (210 kg) aggregate

Tools

- Tape measure, straight-edge and a piece of chalk
- String line and pegs
- Wheelbarrow and bucket
- Spade and shovel
- Sledgehammer
- Wooden battens: several, long enough to edge both sides of the path, about 60 mm wide and 30 mm thick (formwork)
- Tamping beam: about 1 m long, 60 mm wide and 30 mm thick
- Bricklayer's trowel
- Mortar float
- Spirit level
- Piece of railway sleeper or something similar, measuring approximately 400 mm long
- Angle grinder with a stone-cutting disk
- Bolster chisel
- Club hammer
- Broom

UP THE GARDEN PATH

Our path is 5 m long, but the measurements of your garden will probably dictate a different length. Work out how long your path needs to be, divide our quantities by five to give you the amounts for a metre run, and then change the amounts to suit your requirements. Use the tape measure and string line to set out the path on the ground, and then stand back and see how it looks in relation to the site. There are various things to take into consideration before you start the procedure of digging out the earth to a depth of 150 mm, spreading a 60 mm layer of compacted hardcore in the hole and topping it off with a 60 mm layer of concrete. Where are you going to put all the earth? Where are you going to put the hardcore, sand and cement when they are delivered? How are you going to get to and from the house while you are waiting for the cement to cure? You need to decide well in advance. Finally, you need to think about costs and quality. For example, we have kept costs down by using concrete slabs, but you might prefer to use top-quality materials such as stone or ceramic.

CROSS-SECTION OF THE DECORATIVE VICTORIAN PATH

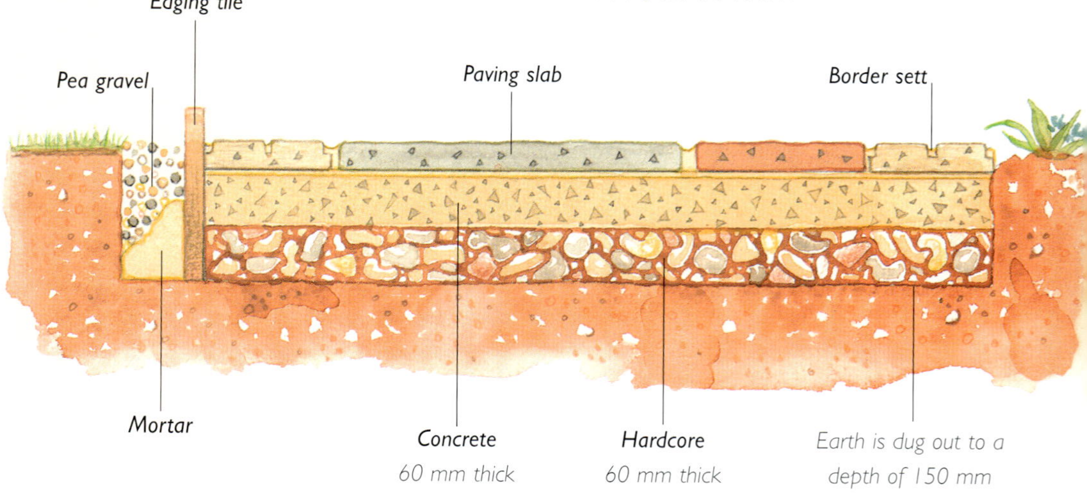

Decorative Victorian path

PLAN VIEW OF THE DECORATIVE VICTORIAN PATH

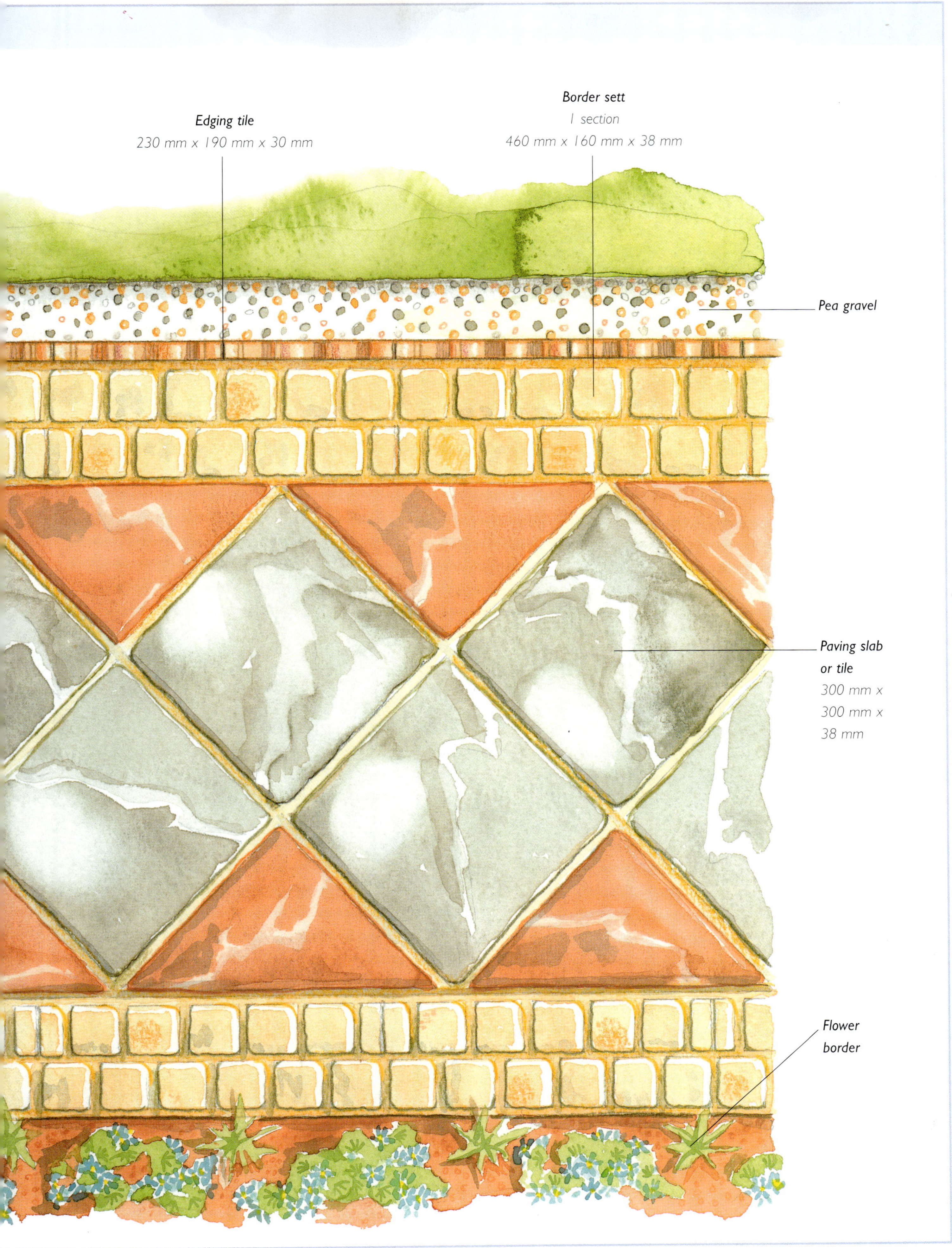
Edging tile
230 mm x 190 mm x 30 mm
Border sett
1 section
460 mm x 160 mm x 38 mm
Pea gravel
Paving slab
or tile
300 mm x
300 mm x
38 mm
Flower
border

Step-by-step: **Making the decorative Victorian path**

Concrete
Avoid damaging the fragile edge of the concrete

Formwork
When the concrete has set, remove the formwork by tapping it away from the concrete

1 Using string and pegs, set out the dimensions of the path (5 m long and 950 mm wide). Remove the earth to a depth of 150 mm, lay a 60 mm layer of hardcore and compact it with the sledgehammer. Build the formwork. Fill with a 60 mm layer of concrete, and tamp level with the top of the formwork.

Bedding the setts
Use the handle of the trowel to tap the border setts into position

Border setts
Bed the setts on to a generous layer of mortar

Concrete
Scrape up any blobs of mortar that drop on the concrete

2 Arrange all the slabs and border setts (dry) on the concrete, just to check that your calculations are correct. Next, mix a wheelbarrow load of mortar and cement the border setts in place, positioning them so that they are flush with the edge of the concrete. Check that they are level with the spirit level.

Club hammer
Give the chisel repeated taps with the club hammer

Bolster chisel
Set the bolster chisel in the scored groove

3 Trim slabs as required. With the slab positioned on the railway sleeper, draw a chalk guideline from corner to corner. Score the line with the angle grinder, set the edge of the bolster chisel in the scored groove, and tap with the club hammer until the slab breaks in half.

Tiles
Wet the tiles prior to bedding them in the mortar

Mortar
The mortar needs to be a loose, wet mix

Bedding
Ease the tile from side to side in order to bed it in the mortar

4 Use the trowel to spread a layer of mortar over the concrete. One at a time, dip the slabs in water, shake off the excess, and then very carefully bed them in place on the mortar. Check that they are level with the spirit level.

Club hammer
Tap the edging tiles into the mortar with the handle of the club hammer

Joints
To achieve uniform joints, ease the tiles apart

Edging tiles
Align the top of the tiles with the top of a 30 mm-thick batten placed on the border setts

5 When the mortar has set, use the spade and trowel to dig a trench 60 mm wide and 150 mm deep alongside the edge of the path. Shovel a generous amount of mortar into the trench, position the edging tiles and tap them level with the handle of the club hammer. When the mortar has set, top the edging trench with pea gravel.

Dry-mix mortar
Brush the dry mortar into all the joints

6 Make a dry-mix mortar consisting of 1 bucketful of cement powder to 3 parts sand, and sweep it carefully backwards and forwards over the path until all the joints are filled. Finally, spray a fine mist of water over the path and leave for 24 hours before walking on it.

Helpful hint

Before you start mixing and brushing the dry-mix mortar, check that the path is absolutely bone dry. If the slabs are damp, or if it looks likely to rain before you complete the task, wait for a dry day.

Railway sleeper steps

Steps made out of railway sleepers are a good, practical idea, because the chunks of wood make really safe and comfortable steps. The combination of wood and stone in this design harmonize together beautifully, but the best thing about the whole structure is that it can be built without concrete. If you have a place where you need a flight of three or four steps, this the project for you.

TIME

A day (four hours for preparing the site, and the rest of the time for placing the wood and the stone).

SPECIAL TIP

Start by obtaining the sleepers, and then modify the width of the steps to fit – perhaps each sleeper can be halved to make two steps.

CROSS-SECTION OF THE RAILWAY SLEEPER STEPS

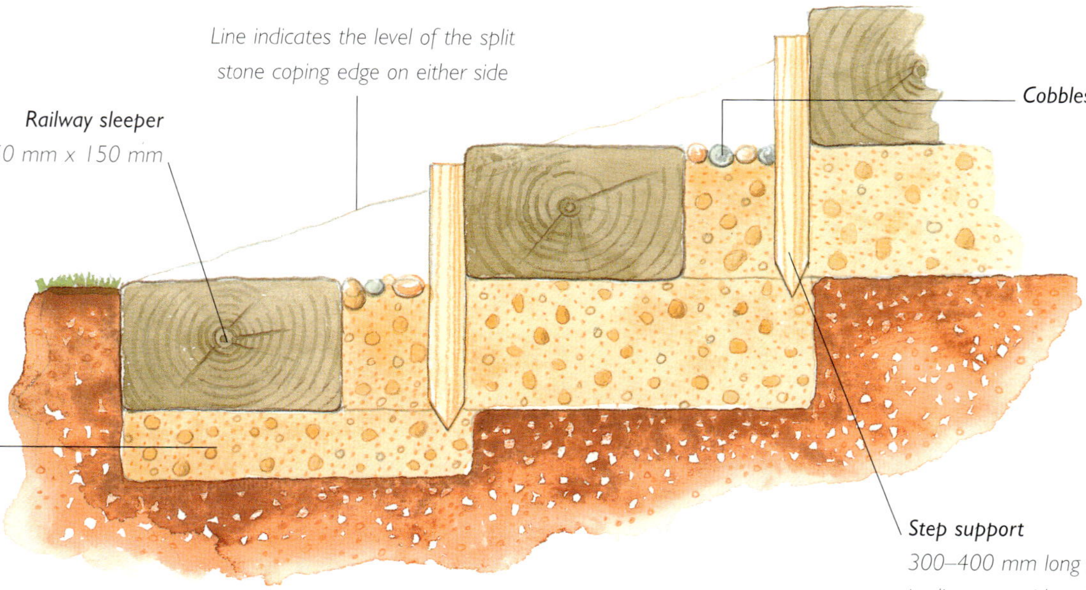

YOU WILL NEED

Materials *for a flight of 4 steps rising 600 mm, 640 mm wide and 2.4 m long*

- Railway sleeper: 4 pieces, 640 mm long, 250 mm wide and 150 mm thick (steps)
- Poles: 8 split, pointed pine poles, about 300–400 mm long and 75 mm in diameter (step supports)
- Ballast: 4 bucketfuls per step
- Cobbles: 1 bucketful per step
- Builder's or soft sand: 1 bucketful per step
- Split stone (sandstone or limestone): approximately 20 plate-size stones for each step (edging)

Tools

- Tape measure
- Spade
- Wheelbarrow and bucket
- Shovel
- Sledgehammer
- Spirit level
- Club hammer
- Hand-sized block of wood
- Mason's hammer

REACHING NEW LEVELS

These steps are built within an existing rockery. However, you could also run the steps up a steep, sloping lawn, as long as they can be cut into an existing mound where the surrounding earth provides plenty of support. It's a marvellously simple system. The first step is bedded on ballast so that it is level with the lawn, more ballast is shovelled behind the sleeper, the second sleeper is positioned and held in place with the step supports, more ballast is shovelled into place, and so on. And as the steps climb up, so the space between one step and another is packed out with cobbles bedded in sand, while the bank at each side of the steps is edged with a coping of split stone. The slow rise in height from one step to another, plus the long depth to the tread, make for ease of use.

If you are making more steps than we have specified in this project, sit down with a pencil and paper and work out the most economical way to use the sleepers – it makes sense to get a number of whole steps out of each sleeper so there is no wastage. Most suppliers will cut sleepers to length if required.

Step-by-step: **Making the railway sleeper steps**

Ballast
Use the sledgehammer to compact the ballast

Levelling
The sleeper needs to be level along its length but tilted slightly forwards for drainage

Ballast
Some builders sell a mix of clay and crushed stone

1 Dig out the earth so that you have a recess about 225 mm deep, 650 mm wide, and 600 mm from front to back. Put a 75 mm-thick layer of ballast in the recess and lay the first sleeper so that it is level with the lawn.

Cobbles
Fit the cobbles so that they are packed closely together

2 Spread a 150 mm layer of ballast to the far side of the first sleeper and set the second sleeper in position. Check with the spirit level. Use the club hammer to bang in two step supports to hold the second sleeper in place. Fill the area between the two sleepers with cobbles and a thin layer of sand.

Helpful hint

Use a watering can to dampen the cobbled area, so that the sand runs into all the nooks and crannies. Repeat this procedure after a few days to make sure the stones are tightly wedged in place.

Compacting block
Beat the surface level with a block of wood

Ballast
If the ballast is hard and dry, you might need to dampen it slightly

Step supports
Angle the poles back so that they are pushing against the sleepers

3 If you find that the ground is especially soft, or there are unexpected cavities to fill, add more ballast and spend extra time beating it firm and level with the sledgehammer. The block of wood makes a good compacting and levelling tool.

Step supports
Remove all traces of bark from the split poles

Cobbles
Positioned so that half of each cobble is in the ground

4 When you are banging in the step supports with the club hammer, make sure that they are pushed hard up against the leading edge of the sleeper, with the top of the pole banged down so that it is just below the level of the step.

Mason's hammer
A mason's hammer is the perfect tool for splitting and shaping the sandstone

Wedge stones
Bang small slivers of stone between the coping stones

Coping stones
Arrange the stones so that there are no sharp points near the steps

5 Dig out a trench at each side of the steps and push a row of vertical coping stones into the earth to hold the whole structure in place. Tap extra stones into the cavities with the mason's hammer, to wedge the whole stack firmly.

Semicircular herb walk

A blend of plain roofing tiles, traditional red bricks and crushed stone chippings make this path a great decorative feature, especially when married with a miniature herb garden. The chippings are hard-wearing and good-looking, but for cats and dogs they are slightly uncomfortable to walk on – perfect if you want to protect your herbs! We have used different coloured chippings in each section to add interest.

TIME

A weekend (one day for preparing the site and setting out the tiles, and the rest of the time for spreading the chippings, planting and tidying up).

SPECIAL TIP

Don't strain your back trying to lift a 50 kg bag of stone chippings to the site. It's much better to open the bag and move the contents one bucketful at a time.

YOU WILL NEED

Materials *for a herb walk 560 mm wide, 3 m in diameter overall, with a 1.5 m radius*

- Plain roof tiles: 50 tiles, 265 mm long and 165 mm wide – this number allows for wastage (path edgings)
- York stone: 7 reconstituted stone coping stones, 450 mm long, 185 mm wide and 47 mm thick (edging for back of semicircle)
- Bricks: 4 bricks, 215 mm long, 102.5 mm wide and 65 mm thick (path divisions)
- Crushed stone chippings: 3 x 50 kg bags in colour(s) of your choice
- Plastic sheet: 6 m long and 1 m wide
- Mortar: 2 parts (30 kg) cement, 1 part (15 kg) lime, 9 parts (135 kg) builder's or soft sand

Tools

- Tape measure, wooden pegs and string
- Club hammer
- Spade and shovel
- Wheelbarrow
- Bucket
- Bricklayer's trowel
- Pointing trowel

A VERY TASTY GARDEN PATH

This project is a very simple affair, really no more than a semicircular path edged with roofing tiles and sub-divided with bricks, with the resultant recesses filled with crushed stone. We used two wooden pegs joined with string to draw out a half-circle. This device was also used to scribe around the circumference to divide the path into three equal sections. We chose to build a semicircle because we wanted to butt it on to the side of an existing path, but you can build a complete circle by doubling up the materials.

The path enables you to nip out from the kitchen and gather herbs to add to your cooking without getting your feet wet or muddy in the garden. The width and depth of the path are also an advantage if you are planting herbs with invasive root systems, such as mint, because the path provides a barrier between the plants and the garden. An ideal feature for a small town garden.

CROSS-SECTION OF THE SEMICIRCULAR HERB WALK

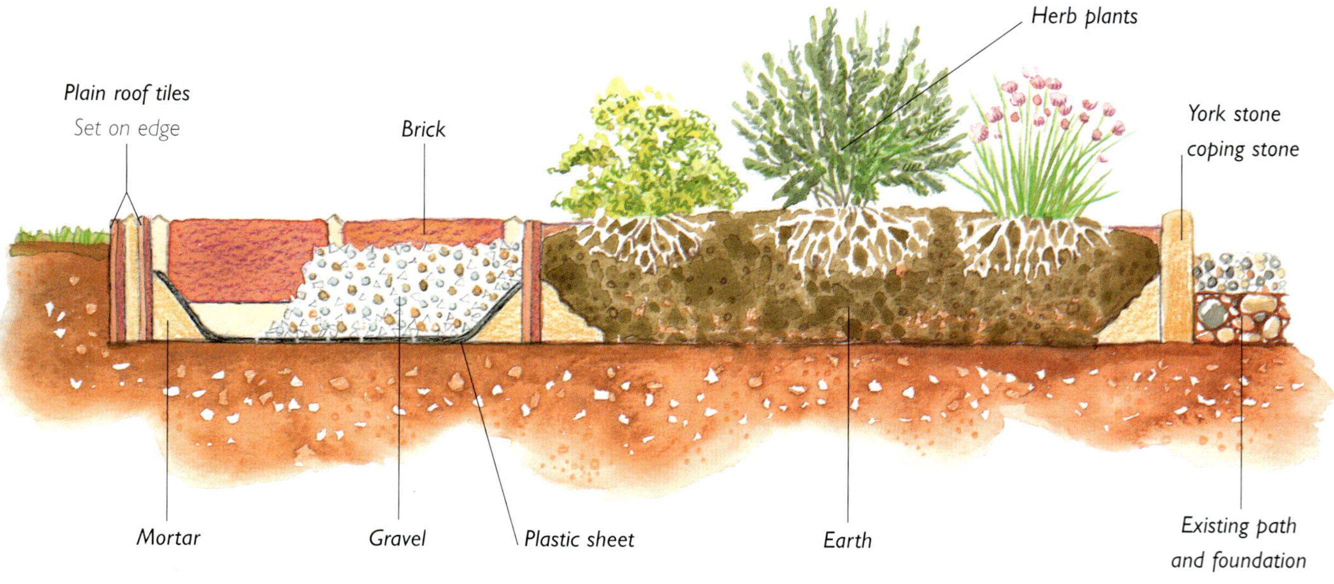

Semicircular herb walk

PERSPECTIVE VIEW OF THE SEMICIRCULAR HERB WALK

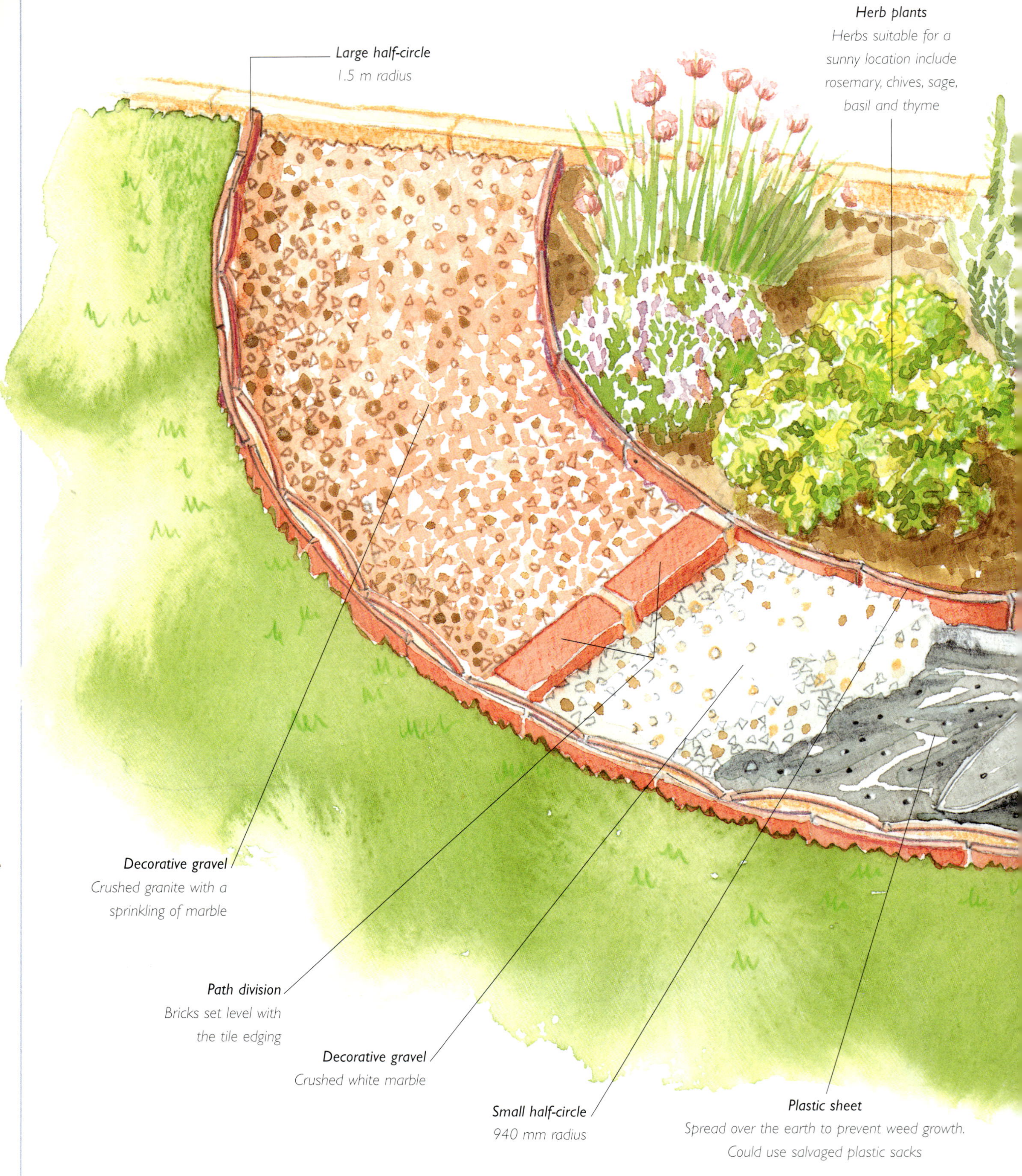

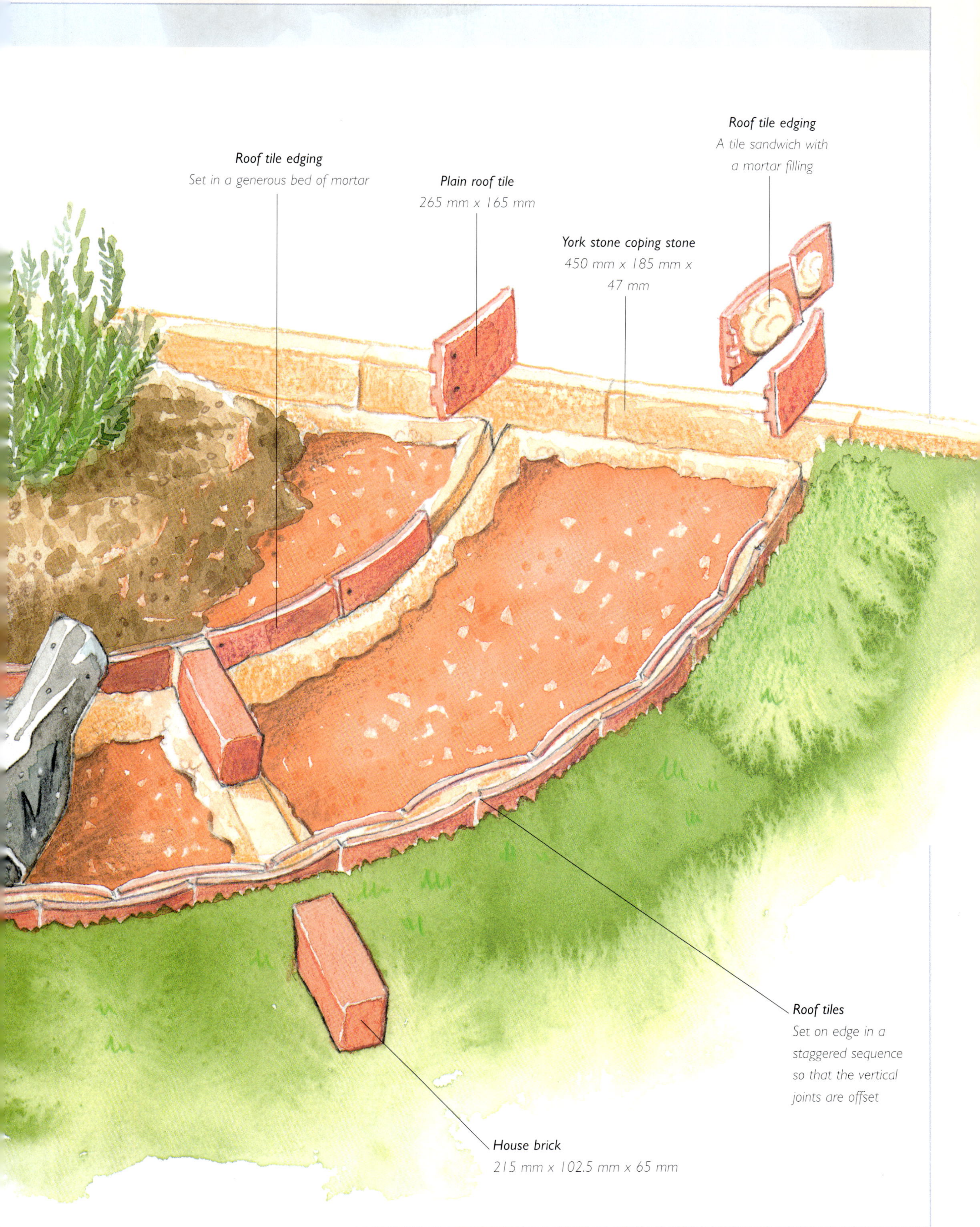
Roof tile edging
Set in a generous bed of mortar
Plain roof tile
265 mm x 165 mm
York stone coping stone
450 mm x 185 mm x 47 mm
Roof tile edging
A tile sandwich with a mortar filling
Roof tiles
Set on edge in a staggered sequence so that the vertical joints are offset
House brick
215 mm x 102.5 mm x 65 mm

Step-by-step: **Making the semicircular herb walk**

Scribing
Use a 1.5 m radius to scribe the circumference of the large circle; also to divide it into three equal parts

Path
The path is 560 mm wide

Small half-circle
Use a radius of 940 mm to set out the small half-circle

1 Take two wooden pegs and tie them together with string so that they are 1.5 m apart. Tap one into the ground (in what will be the centre of the back of the semicircle) with the club hammer. Use the string as a radius to draw out a half-circle 3 m in diameter. Remove the turf to a depth of 150 mm. Repeat the procedure to draw a half-circle with a 940 mm radius within this.

Outer ring
Set the outer ring of tiles with the best face facing outwards

2 Set a single line of roof tiles in mortar around the two circumferences, using the bricklayer's trowel for moving the mortar and the pointing trowel for fine detailing.

Helpful hint

We have used relatively expensive plain roof tiles for the edging, but you could cut costs by using salvaged tiles and slates or even a totally different material such as broken brick, wine bottles set upside down, found rocks or broken paving slabs.

Tamping
Tap the tiles level with the handle of the club hammer

Tile sandwich
The cavity between the tiles is filled with mortar

3 Butter mortar on the inside face of the outer edging of tiles, and run another line of tiles alongside the first so that the edging is two tiles thick. The tiles are placed so that the concave surfaces are facing each other.

Mortar
Use spare mortar to buttress the tiles on the path side

Brick
Set the bricks on edge so that the best face is uppermost

Pointing
Use the point of the small trowel to tidy up the mortar in the tile sandwich

4 Position the York stone slabs to make an edging for the back of the semicircle, and mortar in place. Make the path divisions by setting the bricks on a generous bank of mortar, so that they are aligned with the centre of the circle.

Gravel
Spread an even layer of gravel over the plastic

5 Spread the plastic sheet over the three recessed areas. Cover the plastic with chippings, bringing the level of the path up to within 20 mm of the top of the tile edging. Plant up the central area with herbs.

Herbs
Fill the central area with soil and plant with your favourite culinary herbs

Crazy-paved circular patio

A large, formal circular stone patio is a practical and pleasing garden feature. Small children love to use it for playing games, it offers a good surface for bench seats and picnic tables, it is great for displaying containers of plants, and the strong circular motif provides a counterbalance to informal areas of planting.

TIME

A weekend (about eight hours to remove the lawn and position the edging, and the rest of the time for laying the stone and for pointing).

SPECIAL TIP

The cutting of the stone results in a lot of sharp edges and splinters, so wear gloves and goggles.

YOU WILL NEED

Materials *for a patio 3.02 m in diameter*

- Antique radius brick edging: 16 x 610 mm units (designed to go round the outer edge of a paved circle 2.7 m in diameter)
- Border radius setts (concrete Victorian-style paving stone setts): 20 sections about 500 mm long, 160 mm wide and 38 mm thick (designed to go round the inner edge of a paved circle 2.7 m in diameter)
- Sandstone (split stone in random-size pieces): about 7 sq. m (this amount allows for wastage and choice)
- Formwork: 1 sheet of the thinnest and cheapest grade of plywood, 2.4 m x 1.22 m, cut across the grain to make strips about 200 mm wide
- Hardcore (builder's rubble or waste stone): about 6 wheelbarrow loads
- Sharp sand: about 500 kg
- Concrete:
  1 part (100 kg) cement,
  2 parts (200 kg) sharp sand,
  3 parts (300 kg) aggregate
- Mortar:
  1 part (30 kg) cement,
  2 parts (60 kg) builder's or soft sand

Tools

- Tape measure, wooden pegs and string
- Spade
- Fork
- Wheelbarrow
- Shovel
- Rake
- Saw
- Club hammer
- Bricklayer's trowel
- Length of board to use as a treading board, to spread your weight
- Spirit level
- Length of railway sleeper to use as a worksurface
- Mason's hammer

GOING ROUND IN CIRCLES

The ground in our garden is both wet and sloping, so we decided that once the hardcore and sand for the foundation of the patio was in place, we would start by setting the antique brick edging on a solid concrete base. This meant that the built-up edging would not only contain and stabilize the stone paving, but once the concrete had set, it would also give us a level to work to.

It is best to start by roughly laying out the stones dry, to check that their positions are as you want them, placing the largest pieces more or less at the centre of the circle. Work outwards from the centre, to minimize treading on the stones that are in place. The stones are then bedded in a thick mix of concrete, rather than mortar. All you do is shovel a heap of concrete on the sand, then bed and level the dampened stones in the concrete.

CROSS-SECTION OF THE CRAZY-PAVED CIRCULAR PATIO

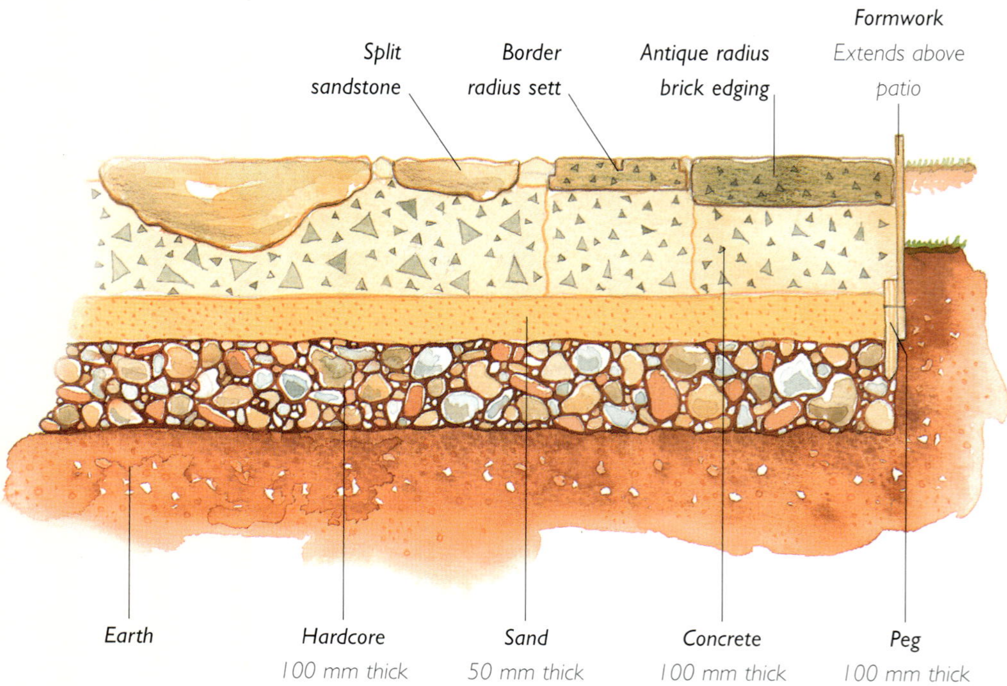

Inspirations: Patios

A patio can transform a garden. If replacing a patch of lawn or some flower beds with a patio seems like a sacrifice, remember that it will help you get more use out of the garden. A patio can become the focus for family gatherings, barbecues or drinks parties. The choice of designs and materials is almost limitless, and a patio can even incorporate small planting pockets to break up a large expanse of stone.

LEFT This charming walled garden has a patio made from a mix of new and salvaged flagstones. The whole structure is elevated on a brick plinth, which creates the stepped or terraced effect and adds interest to a small space.

ABOVE A classic English patio made from salvaged bricks and granite road setts. Note that the bricks follow a grid. The design allows setts to be left out so that low-growing rockery plants can take their place.

RIGHT A traditional country cottage patio of flagstones and half-bricks, with some planting pockets. Thyme is especially suitable for inclusion, as it will survive being walked on and will also release its fragrance.

Snake-pattern cobble path

If you want to build a path that will withstand a lot of use and can cope with children riding on bicycles or skateboards, yet at the same time is decorative, this may be the project for you. Built on a hefty concrete slab, the snake wiggles its way through a cobbled landscape bordered by red bricks – perfect for a modern garden.

TIME

Two weekends (two days for putting down the concrete foundation and laying the bricks, and two days for bedding the setts and cobbles).

SPECIAL TIP

Try to distribute the range of cobbles (according to size and colour) throughout the length of the path.

YOU WILL NEED

Materials *for a path 3 m long. (This path consists of three frames. Quantities have been given for single frames, so you can increase the length of the path if desired.)*

- Border radius setts (concrete Victorian-style paving stone setts): 2 sections, about 500 mm long, 160 mm wide and 38 mm thick, for each 1 m-long frame (designed to go round the inner edge of a paved circle 2.7 m in diameter)
- Bricks: about 15 bricks, 215 mm long, 102.5 mm wide and 65 mm thick (for each 1 m-long frame)
- Hardcore (builder's rubble or waste stone): about 2 wheelbarrow loads for each frame
- Formwork: wooden battens long enough to edge both sides of the path, about 60 mm wide and 30 mm thick
- Gravel (small-size, washed): about 2 bucketfuls for each frame
- Aggregate: about 1 wheelbarrow load for each frame
- Concrete: 1 part (25 kg) cement, 2 parts (50 kg) sharp sand, 3 parts (75 kg) aggregate (approximate amounts for each frame)
- Mortar: 1 part (10 kg) cement, 2 parts (20 kg) builder's or soft sand (approximate amounts for each frame)

Tools

- Tape measure and chalk
- String line and pegs
- Club hammer
- Spade
- Shovel
- Wheelbarrow and bucket
- Sledgehammer
- Tamping beam: about 1 m long, 60 mm wide and 30 mm thick
- Bricklayer's trowel
- Rake

MORE THAN JUST A PATH

This path is three frames long, but quantities have been given for single frames, so that you can easily increase the length of your chosen path. The building process is spread over a two-weekend period. The concrete foundation is put down on the first Saturday, the bricks are laid the next day when the concrete has set, and the lengthy task of positioning the setts and cobbles takes place the following weekend. As the path is presented as a series of frames – just like pictures – you could, if you so wish, complete the project frame by frame and spread it over a much longer period. It is also possible to work harder and get the project finished in a continuous three- or four-day period, but there is no escaping the fact that you do have to wait for the concrete and mortar to set. If you decide to build a path longer than three frames, it is wise to have a small expansion gap between each frame.

CROSS-SECTION OF THE SNAKE-PATTERN COBBLE PATH

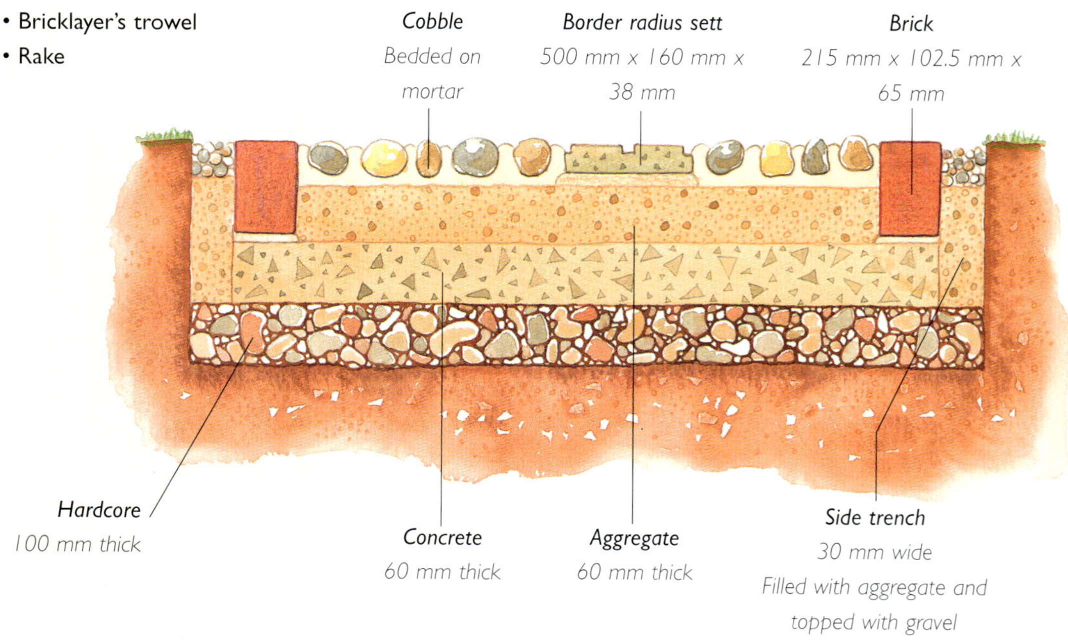

Step-by-step: **Making the snake-pattern cobble path**

Path foundation
Dig out the earth to a depth of 300 mm

Trench
Dig the trench 885 mm wide

1 Use the tape measure, string, club hammer and pegs to set out the path, making it 885 mm wide. Dig out the earth to a depth of about 300 mm. Put a 100 mm layer of hardcore in the recess and hit it level with the sledgehammer.

Tamping
Tamp the concrete level and be sure to remove air bubbles

Concrete
Fill the formwork with 60 mm of concrete

Grass
Try not to drip concrete on the grass

2 Set the formwork battens on edge along the edge of the path (825 mm apart), using the club hammer to knock in pegs to hold them in position. Fill the formwork with concrete to a depth of 60 mm and level it with the tamping beam. Keep tamping until all air bubbles have come to the surface. Leave to set.

Brickwork
Use the small trowel to point the joints between the bricks

Side trench
Fill the side trench with 120 mm of aggregate and top with gravel

3 Remove the formwork. Use the tape measure, chalk and one of the formwork battens to draw out the position of the bricks. Using the bricklayer's trowel, set the bricks on a bed of mortar. Fill the gap between the bricks and the lawn (side trench) with 120 mm of aggregate and top with gravel.

Aggregate
60 mm of aggregate raked over the concrete and levelled

Compacting
Tamp the aggregate level with the sledgehammer

Registration marks
Draw a chalk mark on the brick to show the position of the setts

4 Rake a 60 mm layer of aggregate over the concrete and tamp it level. Position the setts (dry) on the raked aggregate and draw small chalk registration marks on the brick edging so that you know precisely where they need to be placed. Do this with all three frames.

Setts
Bed the setts on a generous spread of mortar

Hammer
Use the weight of the club hammer to nudge the setts into place

Levelling
Level the setts with the top face of the bricks

5 Bed the setts on mortar, so that the curve of the snake runs smoothly from one frame to another. Gently ease the setts from side to side until you are satisfied with the arrangement. Make sure that the setts are level with the bricks.

Cobbles
Ease the cobbles into the mortar until they are level with the bricks

6 Spread and smooth a layer of mortar over the rest of the frame and bed the cobbles in place. You might need to remove some of the mortar to make way for the cobbles.

Helpful hint

The secret of fixing cobbles firmly in place is to dampen them slightly before easing them into the mortar. Sink the cobbles until about half their bulk is hidden in the mortar. If you do not sink the cobbles far enough, they will soon come loose.

Raised decking

Raised decking is particularly appropriate for gardens that are wild and wooded, or where the ground is uneven, or those that back on to water. This type of decking can provide a vantage point and, depending on its situation, the experience can be rather like being in a treehouse, or high up on a wildlife observation platform.

TIME

Two weekends (one day for clearing the ground and sorting out your materials, one day for setting up the basic frame; the second weekend for fitting the banisters and details).

SPECIAL TIP

When you are setting up the main frame, make sure that it is both stable and square. Don't be tempted to rush.

YOU WILL NEED

Materials *for raised decking 2.240 m square (All rough-sawn pine pieces include excess length for wastage. Purchase wood that has been pressure-treated with preservative.)*

- Pine: 8 rough-sawn pieces, 3 m long, 75 mm square section (newel posts and joist supports). Length of newel posts will vary according to the slope of your site
- Pine: 9 rough-sawn pieces, 3 m long, 87 mm wide and 40 mm thick (joists and spacers)
- Pine: 18 pieces planed decking board, grooved or plain, 3 m long, 120 mm wide and 30 mm thick (floor)
- Pine: 10 rough-sawn pieces, 3 m long, 50 mm wide and 30 mm thick (banister rails and fixing battens)
- Pine: 3 rough-sawn pieces, 3 m long, 60 mm wide and 30 mm thick (pitch-topped rail capping)
- Pine: 14 rough-sawn pieces, 2 m long, 40 mm wide and 20 mm thick (temporary battens/slender balusters)
- Pine: 5 rough-sawn pieces, 3 m long, 150 mm wide and 20 mm thick (wide fretted balusters and newel post caps)
- Pine: 8 newel post finials, either turned or carved, size and shape to suit
- Zinc-plated coach bolts with washers and nuts to fit: 24 x 120 mm
- Zinc-plated, countersunk cross-headed screws: 300 x 90 mm no. 8, 300 x 75 mm no. 10
- Steel nails: 1 kg x 125 mm x 5.6 mm
- Concrete blocks: 8 blocks (post foundations)
- Hardcore: 2 bucketfuls per post

Tools

- Two portable workbenches
- Pencil, ruler, tape measure, marking gauge and square
- Crosscut saw
- Cordless electric drill with a cross-point screwdriver bit
- Drill bits to fit the sizes of the nails, screws and bolts
- Spade
- Sledgehammer
- Spirit level
- Claw hammer
- Electric jigsaw
- Pair of clamps
- Electric sander

SIDE VIEW OF THE RAISED DECKING

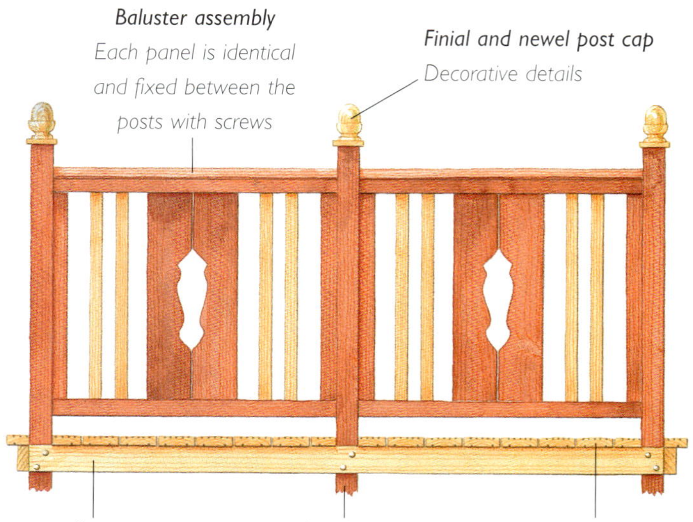

A HIGH-RISE PATIO

The prospect of building raised decking might be a bit daunting, but it is in fact a very straightforward project. We have simplified the main frame by making it as four flat kits – two sides with two corner and one middle newel post each, and two sides with a single middle newel post each. Temporary diagonal battens hold the posts square with each other and stop them twisting during construction. Once the project is in the ground, these are knocked off and used to make the slender balusters.

The structure is a little rickety at first, but once it has been dug in and clenched with bolts, it becomes as firm as a rock. We put spacers between the floor joists. These aren't essential, but because they can be made from offcuts that would otherwise be wasted, and as they take a bit of the bounce out of the floor, we feel that their inclusion is worth the extra time and effort.

Raised decking

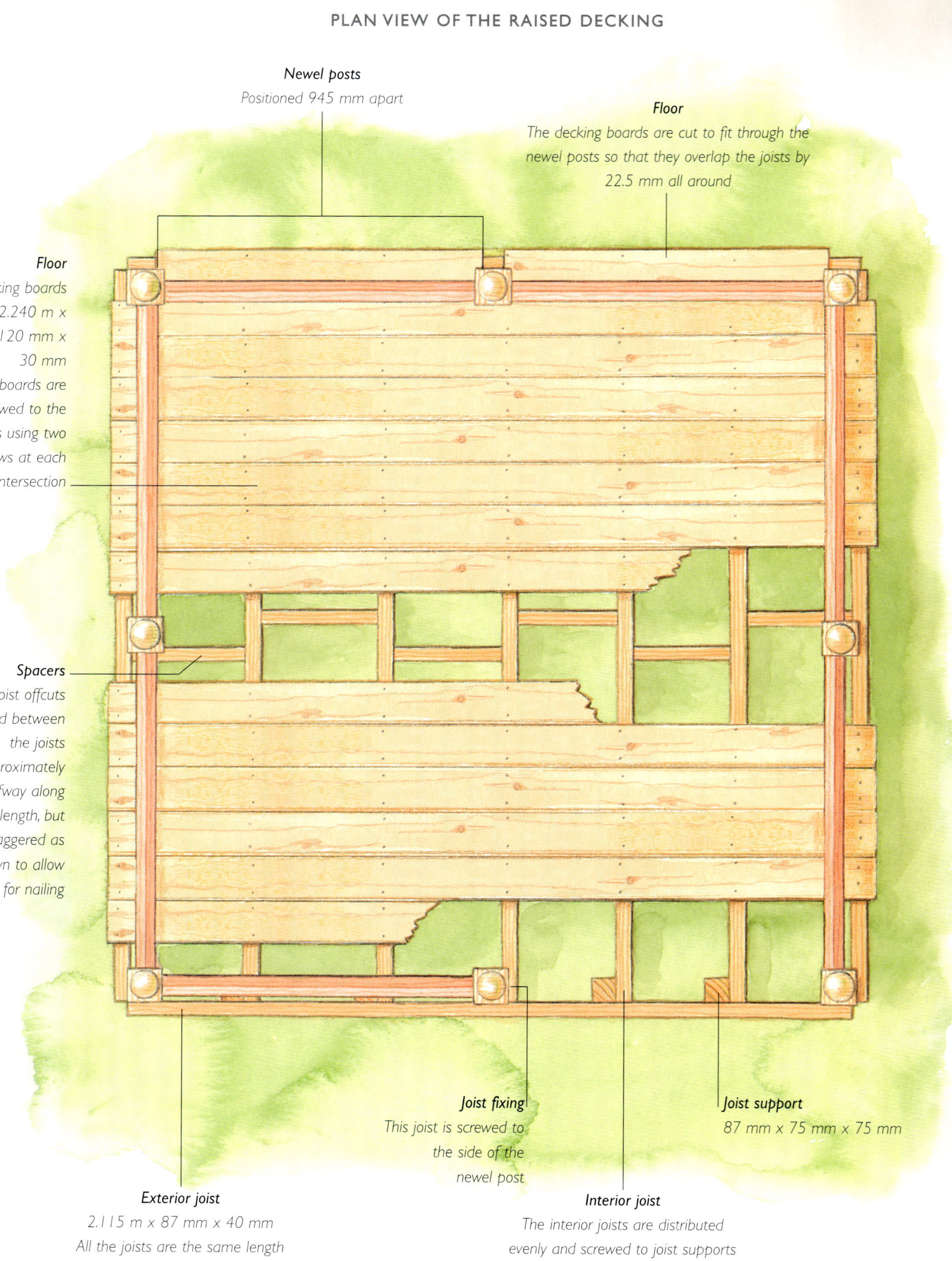

PERSPECTIVE VIEW OF THE RAISED DECKING

Step-by-step: **Making the raised decking**

Newel posts
Set the posts 945 mm apart and square with each other

Joists
The joists need to be bolted 1 m down from the top of the posts

1 Cut the joists to length with the crosscut saw. To make the first side of the main frame, position three newel posts 945 mm apart, with a joist 1 m down from the top, and screw diagonal temporary battens to hold the leg part of the newel posts square. Drill holes and run two bolts through each joist–post intersection. Make an identical second side.

Diagonals
Measure the diagonals – if they are of an identical length, the structure is square

Temporary batten
Fix battens to hold the structure square

Bolts
Clench the bolts tight so that the head of the bolt grips the wood

2 Repeat the procedure described in Step 1 to make the third side of the main frame (only this time, there is a single middle newel post at the centre and no corner posts). Measure the diagonals to confirm that the arrangement is square. Make an indentical fourth side. Link the four sides of the main frame to each other, so that the joists run squarely around it.

Levels
Use the spirit level to check that the structure is level on all sides

3 Bolt the remaining joist ends to the newel posts (reduce the length of the newel posts according to the site). With spade and sledgehammer, set the structure in the ground by digging a hole for each post, placing a concrete block in the bottom, lowering the frame into position, and packing hardcore around the post to hold it in position. Check the levels with the spirit level.

Helpful hint

You will need help putting the structure in position – ideally one person at each side. If you cannot get assistance, assemble in sections using props.

Nailing
Stagger the spacers to allow for nailing

Spacers
Nail offcuts between the joists to prevent the structure from twisting

4 Screw the remaining joists across the main frame. Small, square joist supports are screwed where the exterior and interior joists meet, to strengthen the joist joints. Nail the spacers in a staggered line between the joists, with two nails for each joint. (Nail spacers in a straight line across alternate joists first, and then the offset spacers between remaining joists. Bang in the nails at an angle.)

Screwing
Screw the decking tightly to the joists using one or two screws at each intersection

Decking
Allow 4–8 mm expansion gaps between the decking boards

Overlap
Overlap the boards over the joists all around

5 Starting at the front edge, cut the decking boards for the floor to length and screw them across the run of the joists. Leave a gap of 4–8 mm between boards to allow for expansion.

Spacing
Fix the slender balusters 75 mm away from the fixing battens and the wide fretted balusters

Clamping
Clamp the fixing battens to the newel posts prior to driving in the screws

6 Make up the baluster frames on the ground, complete with fixing battens, top and bottom banister rails, pitch-topped rail capping, wide fretted balusters (shaped with the jigsaw) and slender balusters. Clamp the baluster frames between the newel posts and fix with screws. Screw the newel post caps and finials in position. Finally, sand all the surfaces to a good finish.

Wooden stairway

Dispense with the unattractive piles of concrete blocks or old wooden boxes you've been using as steps, and ascend in style on our attractive rustic stairway. It is designed to fit the Raised Decking on page 114, but the context can be changed.

TIME

A weekend (about eight hours for all the measuring and cutting, and the rest of the time for putting the stairway together).

SPECIAL TIP

When you are at the initial setting-out stage, make sure that you double-check all the angles and measurements.

YOU WILL NEED

Materials *for a five-step stairway, 1.09 m wide. (All rough-sawn pine pieces include excess length for wastage. Purchase wood that has been pressure-treated with preservative.)*

- Pine: 2 pieces of 75 mm square section, 3 m long (back newel posts)
- Pine: 2 pieces of 75 mm square section, 2 m long (front newel posts)
- Pine: 4 pieces, 2 m long, 87 mm wide and 40 mm thick (stringers, stringer supports, step bearer brackets)
- Pine decking boards, grooved or plain: 5 pieces, 2 m long, 120 mm wide and 30 mm thick (stair treads)
- Pine: 6 pieces, 2 m long, 50 mm wide and 30 mm thick (banister rails and fixing battens)
- Pine: 2 pieces, 2 m long, 60 mm wide and 30 mm thick (handrail capping)
- Pine: 6 pieces, 2 m long, 40 mm wide and 20 mm thick (slender balusters)
- Pine: 4 pieces, 2 m long, 150 mm wide and 20 mm thick (wide fretted balusters, step bearers, newel post caps)
- Pine newel post finials: 4 finials, either turned or carved, size and shape to suit
- Zinc-plated coach bolts with washers and nuts to fit: 4 x 120 mm
- Zinc-plated, countersunk cross-headed screws: 100 x 90 mm no. 8, 100 x 75 mm no. 10
- Concrete blocks: 4 blocks (post foundations)
- Hardcore: 1 bucketful per post

Tools

- Pencil, ruler, tape measure, marking gauge and square
- Two portable workbenches
- Crosscut saw
- Cordless electric drill with a cross-point screwdriver bit
- Drill bit to match the sizes of the screws
- Electric sander
- Spade and sledgehammer
- Spirit level
- Electric jigsaw
- Pair of clamps

SIDE VIEW OF THE WOODEN STAIRWAY

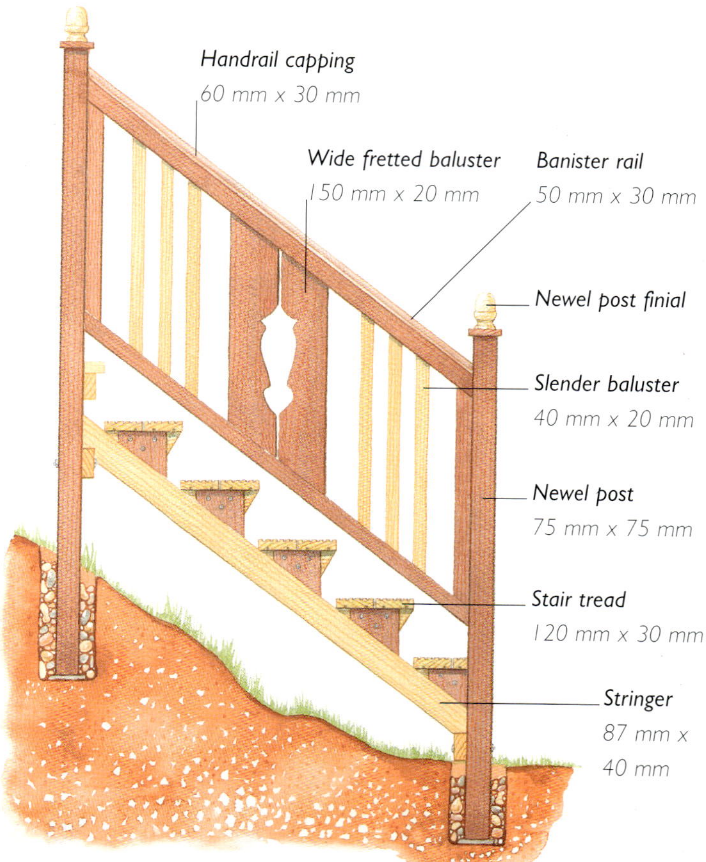

A FLIGHT OF FANCY

If you are going to make these stairs to fit the Raised Decking project on page 114, keep to the sizes and amounts listed. To make alterations such as reducing the number of steps or making them narrower, you need to modify the quantities accordingly.

If you decide to have fewer steps, the angle of the stringer and banister rails stays the same, also the relationship between the height and width of the steps; it's only the details that need to be changed. So if, for example, you want a three-tread design, all the horizontals seen in side view – the banister rails, stringers and handrail capping – will need to be shorter. You will also need to change the design of the balusters (vertical bars).

The best way to proceed, if you simply want to build some steps up to an existing building or structure, is to start by measuring the vertical height from the ground to the doorway or structure. Once you have this measurement, you will be able to decide on the number of steps. It's not always straightforward – for instance, our site was very bumpy, and while we started out with a six-step flight, we decided in the end to bring up the level of the earth and cut down on the number of steps.

Wooden stairway

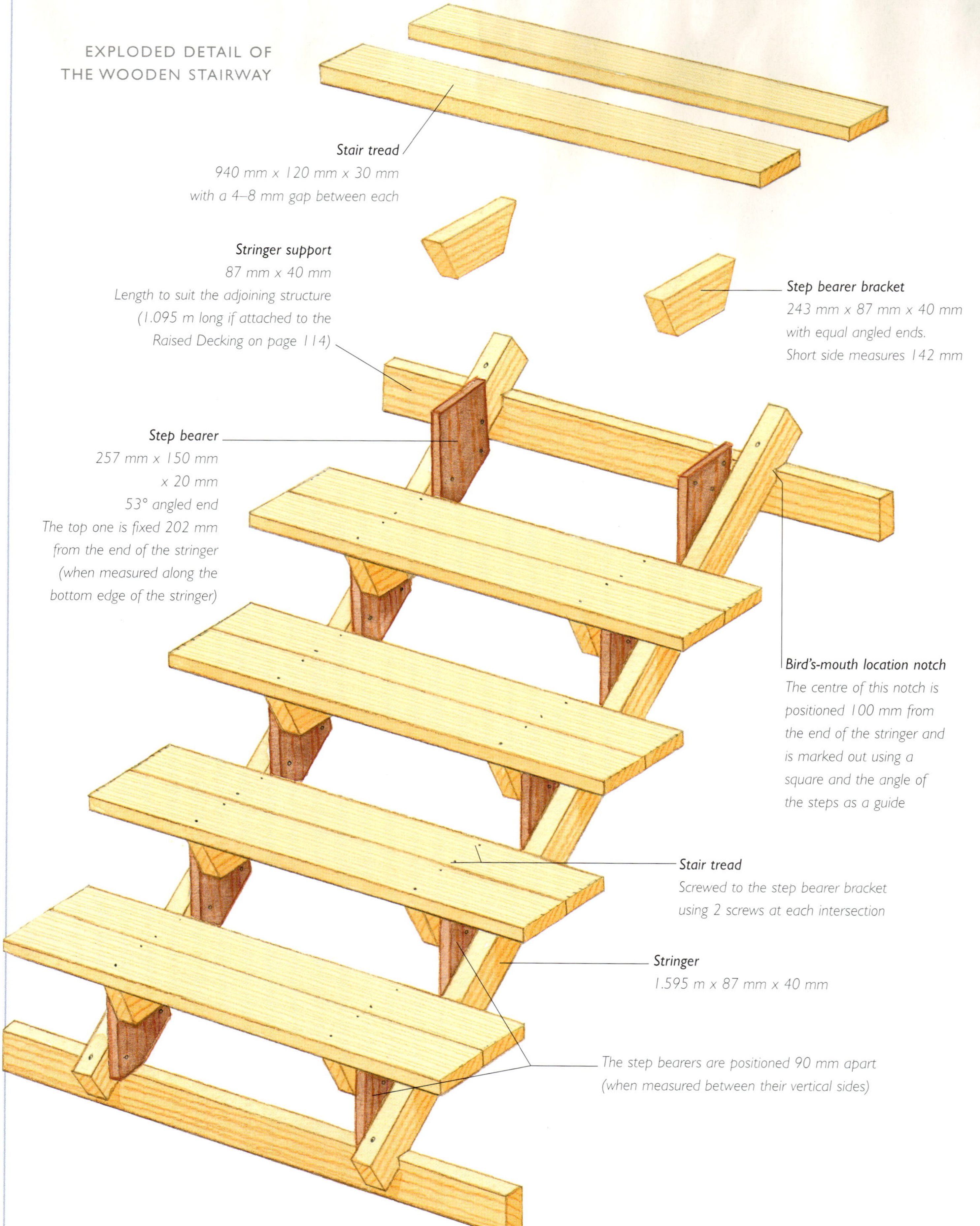

PERSPECTIVE VIEW OF THE WOODEN STAIRWAY
Newel post finial
Size to suit the 75 mm x 75 mm newel post. Screwed to the post cap
Newel post cap
100 mm x 100 mm x 20 mm
Screwed to the top of the newel post
Fixing batten
800 mm x 50 mm x 30 mm
53° angled ends
Handrail capping
60 mm x 30 mm
53° angled ends
Length cut to fit
Wide fretted balusters
800 mm x 150 mm x 20 mm
53° angled ends
Shaped with the jigsaw.
Decorative balusters positioned centrally with a gap of 5 mm between them
Back newel post
3 m x 75 mm x 75 mm
1 m of post extends above the level of the joist
Banister rail
50 mm x 30 mm
53° angled ends
Length cut to fit
Fixing batten
800 mm x 50 mm x 30 mm
53° angled ends
Three screws are used on both sides to fix the assembly to the newel posts
Slender balusters
800 mm x 40 mm x 20 mm
53° angled ends
Front newel post
2 m x 75 mm x 75 mm
1.24 m of post extends above the level of the stringer support
Bird's-mouth location notch
The same shape as the one at the top of the steps, but the centre is positioned 50 mm from the end of the stringer
The ends of the bottom step bearers are cut to stop at the stringer support
Stringer support
Same size as the top stringer support

Step-by-step: **Making the wooden stairway**

1 Take the ten step bearers and step bearer brackets (the 150 mm-wide boards and the 87 mm-wide sections), and fix them together with 75 mm screws. You need two mirror-imaged bearers for each step. Sand them to a splinter-free finish.

2 Cut the two stringers to length. Set the step bearers on the stringers, and use 90 mm screws to fix them in place. Saw bird's-mouth location notches at the ends of the stringers, so they will fit over the stringer supports.

3 Bolt the stringer supports in place on the four newel posts. Set the two stringers in position with the bird's-mouth location notches fitted on the stringer supports, and fix them with 90 mm screws. With spade and sledgehammer, set the structure in the ground by digging a hole for each post (post length may need reducing to suit site), placing a concrete block in the bottom, lowering the frame into position, and packing hardcore around the post to hold it in position. Check that the structure is true with the spirit level.

Screwing
Drill pilot holes prior to fixing the screws

Screwing angle
Run the screws in at an angle to prevent them breaking through the sloped end of the step bearer bracket

4 Cut the ten stair treads to length and fix them in pairs to the step bearer brackets, using 75 mm screws. Use at least two screws for each board end. Fit and fix the balusters, as shown in the raised decking project on pages 114–119 (clamped in place and screwed).

Helpful hint

When you are screwing the stair treads in place, start by fixing the bottom and top steps, so that the structure is square, then fill in with the other steps.

Newel post cap
Run a screw through the centre of the cap and then screw the cap onto the newel post. The central screw is now pointing upwards

5 Cut the newel caps to size and use 75 mm screws to fit them on top of the newel posts. Study the way your chosen finial knobs need to be fixed, and centre them on the newel caps. Finally, rub down the whole structure with the sander to remove splinters and sharp edges.

Newel post finial
Drill a pilot hole in the end of the finial and screw it on to the central newel post cap screw

Glossary

Aligning Setting one component part against another in order to obtain best fit.

Back-filling To fill a cavity (behind a wall or in a foundation trench hole) in order to bring the ground up to the desired level.

Bedding The process of pressing a stone, slab or brick into a bed or layer of wet mortar and ensuring that it is level.

Buttering The act of using a trowel to cover a piece of stone or brick with wet mortar, prior to setting it in position.

Butting The act of pushing one component hard up against another in order to obtain a flush fit, with both faces touching.

Centring Setting a measurement or component part on the centre of another, or measuring a length or width to find the centre.

Cladding Material used to cover a frame (or the process of covering a frame with wood).

Compacting Using a hammer and/or the weight of the body to press down a layer of sand, earth or hardcore.

Courses The horizontal layers of brick or stone within a wall.

Coursing The process of bedding stone and brick in mortar in order to build a course.

Curing time The time taken for mortar or concrete to become firm and stable.

Damping Wetting bricks, slabs or stone prior to bedding them in mortar.

Dressing The act of using a hammer, chisel or trowel to trim a stone to a level, smooth, or textured finish.

Finishing Processes such as sanding, painting, staining, pointing or washing down, which complete a project.

Floating The procedure of using a metal, plastic or wooden float to skim wet concrete or mortar to a smooth and level finish.

Formwork Timber used to support the edges of concrete slabs, paths etc. while the concrete is placed.

Levelling Using a spirit level to decide whether or not a structure or component part is horizontally parallel to the ground, or vertically at right angles to the ground.

Marking out Variously using a pencil, ruler, square, compass, pegs and string to mark out an area.

Pointing Using a trowel, stick or a tool of your choice to bring mortar joints to the desired finish.

Raking out Using a trowel to rake out mortar from between courses, so that edges, bricks or stones are seen to best advantage.

Sighting To determine by eye whether or not a cut, joint or structure is level or true.

Squaring The technique of marking out, with a set square and/or spirit level, so that one surface is at right angles to another.

Tamping The act of using a length of wood to compact and level.

Trimming Bringing wood, brick or stone to a good finish.

Wire brushing Using a wire-bristled brush to remove dry mortar from the face of bricks, slabs or stones, for example on a wall, or the surface of a path or patio.

Suppliers

UK

Tarmac TopPave Ltd
Wergs Hall, Wergs Hall Road
Wolverhampton, Staffordshire
WV8 2HZ
Tel: (01902) 774052
Stockists: (08702) 413450
(Block pavers, decorative pavers, kerbing and edging blocks)

The Natural Stone Co
Elm Cottage, Ockham Road
North Ockham
Woking, Surrey
GU23 6NW
Tel: (01483) 211311

The York Handmade Brick Co
Forest Lane, Alne
York, Yorkshire
YO61 1TU
Tel: (01347) 838881
(Handmade bricks, pavers and terracotta floor tiles)

Sleeper Supplies Ltd
PO Box 1377, Kirk Sandall
Doncaster, Yorkshire
DN3 1XT
Tel: (01302) 888676
(Railway sleepers: new and old/hardwood and softwood)

B & Q plc
1 Hampshire Corporate Park
Chandlers Ford, Eastleigh
Hampshire SO53 3YX
Tel: (01703) 256256

Focus Do-It-All Group Ltd
Gawsworth House
Westmere Drive
Crewe, Cheshire CW1 6XB
Tel: (01384) 456456

Homebase Ltd
Beddington House
Railway Approach, Wallington
Surrey SM6 0HB
Tel: (020) 8784 7200

Wickes
Wickes House
120-138 Station Road
Harrow, Middlesex
HA1 2QB
Tel: (0870) 6089001

SOUTH AFRICA

Bricks, concrete, cement

Cement and Concrete Institute
Portland Park
Old Pretoria Road
Halfway House
Midrand 1685
Tel: (011) 315 0300

Clay Brick Association
PO Box 1284, Halfway House
Johannesburg 1685
Tel: (011) 805 4206

Natal Master Builders' Association Centre
40 Essex Terrace, Westville 3630
Tel: (031) 266 7070

Terraforce
PO Box 1453, Cape Town 8000
Tel: (021) 465 1907
(Retaining blocks)

The Building Centre
Belmont Square, Rondebosch
Cape Town 7700
Tel: (021) 685 3040

Timber

A & L Materials
125 Snapper Road, Wadeville
Johannesburg 1422
Tel: (011) 827 4442

Buffalo Timber
High Street
Ncobo, Queenstown 5050
Tel: (047) 548 1125

Coleman Timbers (Pty) Ltd
Unit 3, 7 Willowfield Crescent
Springfield Park
Durban 4091
Tel: (031) 579 1565

Uitenhage Sawmills
148 Durban Road
Uitenhage 6229
Tel: (041) 922 9920

Valley Timbers
Cnr. Kommetjie and Lekkerwater Roads
Sunnydale, Cape Town 7975
Tel: (021) 785 2684

Stone

Smartstone
101 Retreat Road
Retreat, Cape Town 7945
Tel: (021) 715 7083
(Reconstituted stone products)

Lefarge
Cotswold Street
Port Elizabeth 6001
Tel: (041) 364 3606
(Crushed stone, grit etc.)

AUSTRALIA

ABC Timber & Building Supplies
46 Auburn Road
Regents Park, NSW 2143
Tel: (02) 9645 2511

Banner Timber Centres
191 Main Road
Blackwood SA 5051
Tel: (08) 8278 8211

BBC Hardware
Bld A, Cnr. Cambridge & Chester Streets, Epping
NSW 2121
Tel: (02) 9876 0888

Bowens Timber & Building Supplies
135–173 Macaulay Road
North Melbourne, VIC 3051
Tel: (03) 9328 1041

Bunnings Building Supplies
152 Pilbara Street
Welshpool, WA 6106
Tel: (08) 9365 1555

Elite Paving
33 Neilson Crescent
Bligh Park, NSW 2756
Tel: (4574 1414)

Hudson Timber & Hardware
Cnr. Withers & Milend Roads
Rouse Hill, NSW 2155
Tel: (02) 9629 0488

Pine Rivers Landscaping Supplies
93 South Pine Road
Strathpine, QLD 4500
Tel: (07) 3205 6708

Sydney Stone Yard
1/3A Stanley Road
Randwick, NSW 2031
Tel: (02) 9326 4479

NEW ZEALAND

Masonry

Firth Industries
Freephone: 0800 800 576

Placemakers
Freephone: 0800 425 2269

Stevenson Building Supplies
Freephone: 0800 610 710
(Blocks, bricks, paving, concrete)

Southtile
654 North Road, Invercargill
Tel: (03) 215 9179
Freephone: 0800 768 848
(Tiles and bricks)

Timber merchants

ITM Building Centres
Freephone: 0800 367 486

Rosenfeld Kidson
513 Mt Wellington Highway
Mt Wellington, Auckland
Tel: (09) 573 0503
(Imported and native timber specialists)

Timberline International
71 Foremans Road
Hornby, Christchurch
Tel: (03) 344 2101

Conversion chart

To convert the metric measurements used in this book to imperial measurements, simply multiply the figure given in the text by the relevant number in the table alongside. Bear in mind that conversions will not necessarily work out exactly, and you will need to round the figure up or down slightly. (Do not use a combination of metric and imperial measurements – for accuracy, keep to one system.)

To convert	*Multiply by*
millimetres to inches	0.0394
metres to feet	3.28
metres to yards	1.093
sq millimetres to sq inches	0.00155
sq metres to sq feet	10.76
sq metres to sq yards	1.195
cu metres to cu feet	35.31
cu metres to cu yards	1.308
grams to pounds	0.0022
kilograms to pounds	2.2046
litres to gallons	0.22

Index

A

Angle grinder, 14, 22, 62–67, 82–87
Axe, 13, 17, 25, 34–37, 42–45, 56–61

B

Ballast, 28, 38–41, 42–45, 88–93
Bark chippings, 16, 17, 19, 20, 27, 34, 42–45, 62, 65
Bevel or marking gauge, 12, 114–119, 120–125
Bolts, 13, 17, 25, 114–119, 120–125
Bricks and brickworking techniques, 6, 7, 10, 11, 14, 16, 18, 19, 22, 23, 24, 26, 28, 29, 30, 31, 38–41, 50, 51, 68–72, 76–81, 94–99, 100–105, 108–113

C

Ceramic tiles, 18, 19, 82–87
Chisel, 14, 22, 34–37, 52–55, 62–67, 76–81, 82–87
Clamps and clamping, 13, 114–119, 120–125
Claw hammer, 12, 13, 46–49, 56–61, 114–119
Club hammer, 14, 22, 23, 27, 28, 34–37, 38–41, 46–49, 52–55, 62–67, 68–73, 76–81, 82–87, 88–93, 94–99, 100–105, 108–113
Cobbles, 11, 18, 29, 50, 68–73, 88–93, 108–113
Concrete, 7, 10, 15, 18, 19, 20, 21, 23, 24, 27, 28, 29, 30, 32, 42, 46, 47, 62–67, 68–73, 76–81, 82–87, 100–105, 108–113, 114–119, 120–125
Concrete slabs, 10, 18, 19, 20, 21, 27, 29, 30, 52–55, 62–67, 68–73, 76–81, 82–87, 94–99, 108–113
Crazy paving, 11, 23, 30, 34, 100–105
Crosscut saw, 12, 13, 24, 34–37, 42–45, 56–61, 114–119, 120–125
Cutting
  bricks and stone, 22
  curves in wood, 13, 25
  joints in wood, 25

D

Decking, 11, 16, 17, 20, 25, 27, 28, 29, 31, 34–37, 114–119
Drills and drilling, 13, 25, 34–37, 56–61, 114–119, 120–125

E

Edgings, 16, 17, 18, 19, 20, 26, 28, 31, 38, 46–49, 52–55, 62–67, 82–87, 88–93, 94–99, 100–105, 108–113

F

Formwork, 21, 62–67, 82–87, 100–105, 108-113
Foundations, 12, 14, 20–21, 29, 30, 34, 68–73, 82–87, 94, 100–105, 108–113, 114–119, 120–125

G

Gravel, 18, 19, 27, 30, 31, 34–37, 42–45, 46–49, 50, 64, 82–87, 94–99, 108–113

H

Hardcore, 20, 21, 23, 24, 28, 30, 31, 52, 62–67, 68–73, 82–87, 100–105, 108–113, 114–119, 120–125

J

Jigsaw, 12, 25, 114–119, 120–125

L

Limestone 18, 19, 68–73, 88–93
Log roll border edging, 16, 17, 46–49
Log rings, 16, 46–49

M

Mallet, 13, 25, 34–37, 56–61
Mason's hammer, 14, 88–93, 100–105
Mortar, 7, 14, 19, 20, 21, 22, 23, 28, 30, 62–67, 68–73, 76–81, 82–87, 94–99, 100–105, 108–113

N

Nails and nailing, 13, 17, 21, 24, 25, 29, 56–61, 114–119

P

Paths, 11, 20, 26, 27, 28, 29, 34–37, 46–49, 50–51, 82–87, 94–99, 108–113
Patios, 11, 20, 28, 29, 34–37, 52–55, 62–67, 100–105, 106–107
Planning, 10–11
Plastic sheet, 15, 19, 27, 34–37, 42–45, 46–49, 66, 94–99
Pointing, 14, 23, 73, 76–81, 94–99, 100–105
Posts and poles, 14, 24, 26, 27, 29, 31, 42–45, 56–61, 62–67, 88–93, 114–119, 120–125

R

Railway sleepers, 6, 11, 16, 17, 21, 31, 46, 74, 82–87, 88–93, 100–105
Reconstituted stone, 11, 14, 18, 19, 20, 22, 26, 28, 29, 52–55, 62–67, 82–87, 94–99, 100–105, 108–113
Risers, 21, 30, 31, 42, 74, 76, 80, 81

S

Sand, 10, 14, 15, 18, 19, 20, 21, 22, 23, 27, 28, 29, 34–37, 38–41, 52–55, 62–67, 76–81, 82–87, 94–99, 88–93, 100–104, 108–113
Sawing, 12, 13
Sawn timber sections, 16, 17
Screws and screwing, 13, 17, 21, 24, 25, 29, 114–119, 120–125
Setts, 18, 19, 28, 29, 62–67, 82–87, 100–105, 108–113
Shovel, 15, 19, 28, 34–37, 38–41, 62–67, 68–73, 76–81, 82–87, 88–93, 94–99, 100–105, 108–113
Sledgehammer, 15, 21, 42–45, 56–61, 62–67, 68–73, 82–87, 88–93, 108–113, 114–119, 120–125
Spade, 12, 15, 24, 27, 38–41, 42–45, 46–49, 52–55, 62–67, 68–73, 82–87, 88–93, 94–99, 100–105, 108–113, 114–119, 120–125
Spirit level, 12, 14, 21, 28, 29, 30, 56–61, 62–67, 68–73, 76–81, 82–87, 88–93, 100–105, 114–119, 120–125
Staples, 17, 46–49, 56–61
Stepping stones, 16, 19, 27, 46–49, 51
Steps, 11, 21, 30, 31, 42–45, 68–73, 74–75, 76–81, 88–93, 120–125
Stone, 18, 19, 20, 21, 22, 23, 26, 27, 28, 29, 30, 31, 50, 52–55, 62–67, 68–73, 76–81, 82–87, 88–93, 94–99, 100–105, 106, 107, 108–113

T

Tamping, 21, 28, 34–37, 38–41, 42–45, 62–67, 68–73, 76–81, 82–87, 94–99, 100–105, 108–113
Treads, 21, 30, 31, 42–45, 68–73, 74, 75, 88–93, 120–125
Trowel, 14, 22, 23, 30, 52–55, 62–67, 68–73, 76–81, 82–87, 94–99, 100–105, 108–113

W

Walkways, 11, 25, 26, 27, 56–61
Wheelbarrow, 10, 15, 19, 38–41, 42–45, 46–49, 52–55, 62–67, 68–73, 76–81, 82–87, 88–93, 94–99, 100–105, 108–113
Woodworking techniques, 16, 17, 24–25, 114–119, 120–125

Acknowledgments

AG&G Books would like to thank *Garden and Wildlife Matters Photographic Library* for contributing the pictures used on pages 50 (left), 51 (inset), 74, 75, 106 and 107.